Rick S...

GERMAN

PHRASE BOOK

John Muir Publications
Santa Fe, New Mexico

Thanks to the team of people at *Europe Through the Back Door* who helped make this book possible: Dave Hoerlein, Mary Romano, and...

German translation: Julia Klimek
Phonetics: Risa Laib
Layout: Rich Sorensen
Maps: Dave Hoerlein

Edited by Risa Laib and Rich Sorensen

John Muir Publications, P.O. Box 613, Santa Fe, NM 87504

© 1993, 1995 by Rick Steves
Cover © 1993, 1995 by John Muir Publications
Cover photo by Rick Steves
Second edition. First printing, April 1995
All rights reserved.
Printed in the United States of America
by McNaughton & Gunn

ISBN 1-56261-214-X

Distributed to the book trade by
Publishers Group West
Emeryville, CA

While every effort has been made to keep the content of this book accurate, the author and publisher accept no responsibility whatsoever for anyone ordering bad beer or getting messed up in any other way because of the linguistic confidence this phrase book has given them.

JMP travel guidebooks by Rick Steves:

Rick Steves' Best of Germany, Austria, & Switzerland
Rick Steves' Europe Through the Back Door
Europe 101: History and Art for the Traveler
   (with Gene Openshaw)
Mona Winks: Self-Guided Tours of Europe's Top Museums
   (with Gene Openshaw)
Rick Steves' Best of Europe
Rick Steves' Best of France, Belgium & the Netherlands
   (with Steve Smith)
Rick Steves' Best of Great Britain
Rick Steves' Best of Italy
Rick Steves' Best of Scandinavia
Rick Steves' Best of Spain & Portugal
Rick Steves' Best of the Baltics & Russia (with Ian Watson)
Rick Steves' Phrase Books: French, Italian, German,
   French/Italian/German, and Spanish/Portuguese
Asia Through the Back Door (with Bob Effertz)
Kidding Around Seattle

Rick Steves' company, *Europe Through the Back Door*, provides many services for budget European travelers, including a free quarterly newsletter/catalog, budget travel books and accessories, Eurailpasses (with free video and travel advice included), a free computer BBS Travel Information Line, a travel partners list, intimate European bus tours, and a user-friendly Travel Resource Center in Edmonds, WA. For more information and a free newsletter subscription, call or write to:

Europe Through the Back Door
120 Fourth Avenue N, Box 2009
Edmonds, WA 98020 USA
Tel: 206/771-8303, Fax: 206/771-0833

Contents

Hi, I'm Rick Steves.

I'm the only mono-lingual speaker I know who's had the nerve to design a series of European phrase books. But that's one of the things that makes them better. You see, after twenty summers of travel through Europe, I've learned first-hand (1) what's essential for communication in another country, and (2) what's not. I've assembled these most important words and phrases in a logical, no-frills format, and I've worked with native Europeans and seasoned travelers to give you the simplest, clearest translations possible.

But this book is more than just a pocket translator. The words and phrases have been carefully selected to make you a happier, more effective budget traveler. The key to getting more out of every travel dollar is to get closer to the local people, and to rely less on entertainment, restaurants, and hotels that cater only to foreign tourists. This book will give you linguistic four-wheel drive to navigate through German, Austrian and Swiss culture—from ordering a meal at a locals-only Tirolean restaurant to discussing social issues, travel dreams, and your *wurst* memories with the family that runs the place. Long after your memories of castles and museums have faded, you'll still treasure the close encounters you had with your new European friends.

A good phrase book should help you enjoy your linguistic adventure—not just survive it—so I've added a healthy dose of humor. But please use these phrases carefully, in a self-effacing spirit. Remember that one ugly American can undo the goodwill built by dozens of culturally-sensitive ones.

To get the most out of this book, take the time to internalize and put into practice my German pronunciation tips. I've spelled out the pronunciations as if you were reading English. Don't worry too much about memorizing grammatical rules, like which gender a particular noun is—toss sex out the window and communicate!

German is the closest thing I'll ever have to a "second language." It takes only a few words to feel like I'm part of the greater Germanic family, greeting hikers in the Alps, commiserating over the crowds in Rothenburg, prosting in the beerhalls of Blindenpist, and slap-dancing in Tirol.

You'll notice this book has an English-German dictionary and a nifty menu decoder (to help you figure out what's cooking). You'll also find German tongue twisters, international words, telephone tips, and a handy tear-out "cheat sheet." Tear it out and tuck it into your dirndl or lederhosen, so you can easily use it to memorize key phrases during otherwise idle moments. As you prepare for your trip, you may want to take advantage of my annually-updated *Rick Steves' Best of Germany, Austria & Switzerland* guidebook.

My goal is to help you become a more confident, extroverted traveler. If this phrase book helps make that happen, or if you have suggestions for making it better, I'd love to hear from you.

Happy travels, and *Viel Glück* (good luck) as you hurdle the language barrier!

Rick Steves

Getting Started

Versatile, entertaining German

...is spoken throughout Germany, Austria, and most of Switzerland. In addition, German rivals English as the handiest second language in Scandinavia, the Netherlands, Eastern Europe, and Turkey.

German is kind of a "lego language." Be on the lookout for fun combination words. A *Fingerhut* (finger hat) is a thimble, a *Halbinsel* (half island) is a peninsula, a *Stinktier* (stinky animal) is a skunk, and a *Dummkopf* (dumb head) is . . . um . . . uh . . .

German has some key twists to its pronunciation:

CH sounds like the guttural CH in Scottish loch.
J sounds like Y in yes.
S can sound like S in sun or Z in zoo.
 But *S* followed by *CH* sounds like SH in shine.
V sounds like F in fun.
W sounds like V in volt.
Z sounds like TS in hits.
EI sounds like I in light.
EU sounds like OY in joy.
IE sounds like EE in seed.

German has a few unusual signs and sounds. The letter *ß* is not a letter B at all—it's the sound of "ss." Some of the German vowels are double-dotted with an "umlaut." The *ü* has a sound uncommon in English. To make the *ü* sound, round your lips to say "o," but say "ee." The German *ch* has a clearing-your-throat sound. Say *Achtung!*

Here's a guide to the phonetics in this book:

ah	like A in father.
ay	like AY in play.
e, eh	like E in let.
ee	like EE in seed.
ehr	sounds like "air."
ew	pucker your lips and say "ee."
g	like G in go.
i	like I in bit.
ī	like I in light.
kh	like the guttural CH in Scottish loch.
o	like O in cost.
oh	like O in note.
oo	like OO in too.
ow	like OW in cow.
oy	like OY in joy.
ts	like TS in hits. It's a small explosive sound.
u	like U in put.
ur	like UR in purr.

In German, the verb is often at the end of the sentence—it's where the action is. Germans capitalize all nouns. Each noun has a sex which determines which "the" you'll use (*der* boy, *die* girl, and *das* neuter). No traveler is expected to remember which is which. It's O.K. to just grab whichever "the" (*der, die, das*) comes to mind. In the interest of simplicity, we've occasionally left out the articles. Also for simplicity, we often drop the "please." Please use "please" (*bitte*) liberally.

Each German-speaking country has a distinct dialect. The Swiss speak a lilting Swiss-German but write High German like the Germans. The multilingual Swiss greet you with a cheery *"Gruetzi,"* use *"Merci"* for thank you, and say goodbye with a *"Ciao."* Both Austrians and Bavarians speak in a sing-song dialect, and greet one another with *"Grüss Gott"* (May God greet you).

German Basics

Meeting and greeting Germans:

Good day.	**Guten Tag.**	**goo**-ten tahg
Good morning.	**Guten Morgen.**	**goo**-ten **mor**-gen
Good evening.	**Guten Abend.**	**goo**-ten **ah**-bent
Good night.	**Gute Nacht.**	**goo**-teh nahkht
Hi. (informal)	**Hallo.**	**hah**-loh
Welcome!	**Willkommen!**	vil-**kom**-men
Mr. / Mrs. / Miss	**Herr / Frau / Fräulein**	hehr / frow / **froy**-līn
How are you?	**Wie geht's?**	vee gayts
Very well, thanks.	**Sehr gut, danke.**	zehr goot **dahng**-keh
And you?	**Und Ihnen?**	oont **ee**-nen
My name is...	**Ich heiße...**	ikh **hī**-seh
What's your name?	**Wie heißen Sie?**	vee **hī**-sen zee
Pleased to meet you.	**Sehr erfreut.**	zehr ehr-**froyt**
Where are you from?	**Woher kommen Sie?**	**voh**-hehr **kom**-men zee
I am / Are you...?	**Ich bin / Sind Sie...?**	ikh bin / zint zee
...on vacation	**...auf Urlaub**	owf **oor**-lowp
Are you working today?	**Arbeiten Sie heute?**	**ar**-bīt-en zee **hoy**-teh
See you later!	**Bis später!**	bis **shpay**-ter
So long! (informal)	**Tschüss!**	chewss
Goodbye.	**Auf Wiedersehen.**	owf **vee**-der-zayn
Good luck!	**Viel Glück!**	feel glewk
Have a good trip!	**Gute Reise!**	**goo**-teh **rī**-zeh

Survival Phrases

Patton made it all the way to Berlin by using only these phrases. They're repeated on your tear-out "cheat sheet" near the end of this book.

The essentials:

Good day.	**Guten Tag.**	**goo**-ten tahg
Do you speak English?	**Sprechen Sie Englisch?**	**shprekh**-en zee **eng**-lish
Yes. / No.	**Ja. / Nein.**	yah / nīn
I don't speak German.	**Ich spreche kein Deutsch.**	ikh **shprekh**-eh kīn doych
I'm sorry.	**Entschuldigung.**	ent-**shool**-dee-goong
Please.	**Bitte.**	**bit**-teh
Thank you.	**Danke.**	**dahng**-keh
No problem.	**Kein Problem.**	kīn proh-**blaym**
Very good.	**Sehr gut.**	zehr goot
You are very kind.	**Sie sind sehr freundlich.**	zee zint zehr **froynd**-likh
Goodbye.	**Auf Wiedersehen.**	owf **vee**-der-zayn

Where?

Where is...?	**Wo ist...?**	voh ist
...a hotel	**...ein Hotel**	īn hoh-**tel**
...a youth hostel	**...eine Jugend- herberge**	ī-neh **yoo**-gend- hehr-behr-geh

...a restaurant	...ein Restaurant	īn res-tow-**rahnt**
...a supermarket	...ein Supermarkt	īn **zoo**-per-markt
...a pharmacy	...eine Apotheke	ī-neh ah-poh-**tay**-keh
...a bank	...eine Bank	ī-neh bahnk
...the train station	...der Bahnhof	dehr **bahn**-hohf
...the tourist information office	...das Touristen-informationsbüro	dahs **too**-ris-ten-īn-for-maht-see-**ohns**-bew-roh
...the toilet	...die Toilette	dee toh-**leh**-teh
men / women	Herren / Damen	**hehr**-ren / **dah**-men

How much?

How much is it?	Wieviel kostet das?	vee-**feel kos**-tet dahs
Write it?	Schreiben?	**shrī**-ben
Cheap / Cheaper / Cheapest.	Billig / Billiger / Am Billigsten.	**bil**-lig / **bil**-lig-er / ahm **bil**-lig-sten
Is it free?	Ist es umsonst?	ist es com-**zohnst**
Included?	Eingeschlossen?	**īn**-geh-shlos-sen
Do you have...?	Haben Sie...?	**hah**-ben zee
I would like...	Ich hätte gern...	ikh **het**-teh gehrn
We would like...	Wir hätten gern...	veer **het**-ten gehrn
...this.	...dies.	deez
...just a little.	...nur ein bißchen.	noor in **bis**-yen
...more.	...mehr.	mehr
...a ticket.	...ein Karte.	īn **kar**-teh
...a room.	...ein Zimmer.	īn **tsim**-mer
...the bill.	...die Rechnung.	dee **rekh**-noong

How many?

one	**eins**	īns
two	**zwei**	tsvī
three	**drei**	drī
four	**vier**	feer
five	**fünf**	fewnf
six	**sechs**	zex
seven	**sieben**	**zee**-ben
eight	**acht**	ahkht
nine	**neun**	noyn
ten	**zehn**	tsayn

You'll find more to count on in the Numbers chapter.

When?

At what time?	**Um wieviel Uhr?**	oom vee-**feel** oor
Just a moment.	**Moment.**	moh-**ment**
now / soon / later	**jetzt / bald / später**	yetzt / bahld / **shpay**-ter
today / tomorrow	**heute / morgen**	**hoy**-teh / **mor**-gen

Be creative! You can combine these survival phrases to say:
"Two, please," or "No, thank you," or "I'd like a cheap
hotel," or "Cheaper, please?" Please is a magic word in any
language. If you want something and you don't know the
word for it, just point and say, *"Bitte"* (Please). If you
know the word for what you want, such as the bill, simply
say, *"Rechnung, bitte"* (Bill, please).

Struggling with German:

Do you speak English?	**Sprechen Sie Englisch?**	shprekh-en zee eng-lish
A teeny weeny bit?	**Ein ganz klein bißchen?**	īn gahnts klīn bis-yen
Please speak English.	**Bitte sprechen Sie Englisch.**	bit-teh shprekh-en zee eng-lish
You speak English well.	**Ihr Englisch ist sehr gut.**	eer eng-lish ist zehr goot
I don't speak German.	**Ich spreche kein Deutsch.**	ikh shprekh-eh kīn doych
I speak a little German.	**Ich spreche ein bißchen Deutsch.**	ikh shprekh-eh īn bis-yen doych
What is this in German?	**Wie heißt das auf Deutsch?**	vee hīst dahs owf doych
Repeat?	**Noch einmal?**	nokh īn-mahl
Slowly.	**Langsam.**	lahng-zahm
Do you understand?	**Verstehen Sie?**	fehr-shtay-hen zee
I understand.	**Ich verstehe.**	ikh fehr-shtay-heh
I don't understand.	**Ich verstehe nicht.**	ikh fehr-shtay-heh nikht
Write it?	**Schreiben?**	shrī-ben
Who speaks English?	**Wer kann Englisch?**	vehr kahn eng-lish

Handy questions:

How much?	**Wieviel?**	vee-**feel**
How many?	**Wieviele?**	vee-**fee**-leh
How long...?	**Wie lang...?**	vee lahng
...is the trip	**...dauert die Reise**	**dow**-ert dee **rī**-zeh
How far?	**Wie weit?**	vee vīt
How?	**Wie?**	vee
Is it possible?	**Ist es möglich?**	ist es **mur**-glikh
Is it necessary?	**Ist das nötig?**	ist dahs **nur**-tig
Can you help me?	**Können Sie mir helfen?**	**kurn**-nen zee meer **hehl**-fen
What?	**Was?**	vahs
What is that?	**Was ist das?**	vahs ist dahs
What is better?	**Was ist besser?**	vahs ist **bes**-ser
When?	**Wann?**	vahn
What time is it?	**Wie spät ist es?**	vee shpayt ist es
At what time?	**Um wieviel Uhr?**	oom vee-**feel** oor
On time? Late?	**Pünktlich? Spät?**	**pewnkt**-likh / shpayt
When does this...?	**Um wieviel Uhr ist hier...?**	oom vee-**feel** oor ist heer
...open	**...geöffnet**	geh-**urf**-net
...close	**...geschlossen**	geh-**shlos**-sen
Where is / are...?	**Wo ist / sind...?**	voh ist / zint
Where can I find...?	**Wo kann ich... finden?**	voh kahn ikh... **fin**-den
Do you have...?	**Haben Sie...?**	**hah**-ben zee

Can I...?	**Kann ich...?**	kahn ikh
Can we...?	**Können wir...?**	**kurn**-nen veer
...have one	**...eins haben**	īns **hah**-ben
...go free	**...unsonst rein**	oom-**zohnst** rīn
Who?	**Wer?**	vehr
Why?	**Warum?**	vah-**room**
Why not?	**Warum nicht?**	vah-**room** nikht
Yes or no?	**Ja oder nein?**	yah **oh**-der nīn

To prompt a simple answer, ask, *"Ja oder nein?"* (Yes or no?). To turn a word or sentence into a question, ask it in a questioning tone. An easy way to ask, "Where is the toilet?" is to say, *"Toilette?"*

Das yin und yang:

cheap / expensive	**billig / teuer**	**bil**-lig / **toy**-er
big / small	**groß / klein**	grohs / klīn
hot / cold	**heiß / kalt**	hīs / kahlt
open / closed	**geöffnet / geschlossen**	geh-**urf**-net / geh-**shlos**-sen
entrance / exit	**Eingang / Ausgang**	**īn**-gahng / **ows**-gahng
arrive / depart	**ankommen / abfahren**	**ahn**-kom-men / **ahp**-fah-ren
early / late	**früh / spät**	frew / shpayt
soon / later	**bald / später**	bahld / **shpay**-ter
fast / slow	**schnell / langsam**	shnel / **lahng**-zahm
here / there	**hier / dort**	heer / dort

near / far	**nah / fern**	nah / fehrn
good / bad	**gut / schlecht**	goot / shlekht
best / worst	**beste / schlechteste**	**bes**-teh / **shlekh**-tes-teh
a little / lots	**wenig / viel**	**vay**-nig / feel
more / less	**mehr / weniger**	mehr / **vay**-nig-er
mine / yours	**mein / ihr**	mīn / eer
easy / difficult	**leicht / schwierig**	līkht / **shvee**-rig
left / right	**links / rechts**	links / rekhts
up / down	**oben / unten**	**oh**-ben / **oon**-ten
young / old	**jung / alt**	yoong / ahlt
new / old	**neu / alt**	noy / ahlt
heavy / light	**schwer / leicht**	shvehr / līkht
dark / light	**dunkel / hell**	**dun**-kel / hel
beautiful / ugly	**schön / häßlich**	shurn / **hes**-likh
smart / stupid	**klug / dumm**	kloog / dum
vacant / occupied	**frei / besetzt**	frī / beh-**zetst**
with / without	**mit / ohne**	mit / **oh**-neh

Big little words:

I	**ich**	ikh
you (formal)	**Sie**	zee
you (informal)	**du**	doo
we	**wir**	veer
he	**er**	ehr
she	**sie**	zee
they	**sie**	zee
and	**und**	oont

at	**bei**	bī
because	**weil**	vīl
but	**aber**	**ah**-ber
by (via)	**mit**	mit
for	**für**	fewr
from	**von**	fon
here	**hier**	heer
in	**in**	in
not	**nicht**	nikht
now	**jetzt**	yetst
only	**nur**	noor
or	**oder**	**oh**-der
this / that	**dies / das**	deez / dahs
to	**nach**	nahkh
very	**sehr**	zehr

Handy German expressions:

Stimmt.	shtimt	Correct.
Ach so.	ahkh zoh	I see.
Achtung.	ahkh-toong	Attention.
Prima.	**pree**-mah	Fine.
Genau.	geh-**now**	Exactly.
Es geht.	es gayt	So-so.
Alles klar.	**ah**-les klar	Everything is clear.
Ausgezeichnet.	ows-get-**sīkh**-net	Excellent.
Gemütlich.	geh-**mewt**-likh	Cozy.
Bitte.	**bit**-teh	Please. / Can I help you? / Excuse me. / You're welcome.

German names for places:

Germany	**Deutschland**	**doych**-lahnd
Munich	**München**	**mewnkh**-en
Bavaria	**Bayern**	**bī**-ehrn
Black Forest	**Schwarzwald**	**shvartz**-vahld
Danube	**Donau**	**doh**-now
Austria	**Österreich**	**urs**-tehr-rīkh
Vienna	**Wien**	veen
Switzerland	**Schweiz**	shvītz
Italy	**Italien**	i-**tah**-lee-en
Venice	**Venedig**	**veh**-neh-dig
France	**Frankreich**	**frahnk**-rīkh
Spain	**Spanien**	**shpahn**-ee-en
Netherlands	**Niederlanden**	**nee**-der-lahn-den
England	**England**	**eng**-glahnd
Greece	**Griechenland**	**greekh**-en-lahnd
Turkey	**Türkei**	tewr-**kī**
Europe	**Europa**	oy-**roh**-pah
Russia	**Rußland**	**roos**-lahnd
Africa	**Afrika**	**ah**-free-kah
United States	**Vereinigte Staaten**	fehr-ī-nig-teh **shtah**-ten
Canada	**Kanada**	**kah**-nah-dah
world	**Welt**	velt

Numbers

1	**eins**	īns
2	**zwei**	tsvī
3	**drei**	drī
4	**vier**	feer
5	**fünf**	fewnf
6	**sechs**	zex
7	**sieben**	**zee**-ben
8	**acht**	ahkht
9	**neun**	noyn
10	**zehn**	tsayn
11	**elf**	elf
12	**zwölf**	tsvurlf
13	**dreizehn**	**drī**-tsayn
14	**vierzehn**	**feer**-tsayn
15	**fünfzehn**	**fewnf**-tsayn
16	**sechzehn**	**zekh**-tsayn
17	**siebzehn**	**zeeb**-tsayn
18	**achtzehn**	**ahkht**-tsayn
19	**neunzehn**	**noyn**-tsayn
20	**zwanzig**	**tsvahn**-tsig
21	**einundzwanzig**	**īn**-oont-tsvahn-tsig
22	**zweiundzwanzig**	**tsvī**-oont-tsvahn-tsig
23	**dreiundzwanzig**	**drī**-oont-tsvahn-tsig
30	**dreißig**	**drī**-sig
31	**einunddreißig**	**īn**-oont-drī-sig
40	**vierzig**	**feer**-tsig

41	**einundvierzig**	īn-oont-feer-tsig
50	**fünfzig**	fewnf-tsig
60	**sechzig**	zekh-tsig
70	**siebzig**	zeeb-tsig
80	**achtzig**	ahkht-tsig
90	**neunzig**	noyn-tsig
100	**hundert**	hoon-dert
101	**hunderteins**	hoon-dert-**īns**
102	**hundertzwei**	hoon-dert-**tsvī**
200	**zweihundert**	tsvī-hoon-dert
1000	**tausend**	tow-zend
1996	**neunzehnhundert-sechsundneunzig**	noyn-tsayn-hoon-dert-zex-oont-**noyn**-tsig
2000	**zweitausend**	tsvī-tow-zend
10,000	**zehntausend**	tsayn-tow-zend
million	**Million**	mil-**yohn**
billion	**Milliarde**	mil-**yar**-deh
first	**erste**	ehr-steh
second	**zweite**	tsvī-teh
third	**dritte**	drit-teh
half	**halb**	hahlp
100%	**hundert Prozent**	hoon-dert proh-**tsent**
number one	**Nummer eins**	num-mer īns

The number *zwei* (two) is sometimes pronounced "zwoh" in restaurants, hotels, and phone conversations to help distinguish between the similar sounds of *eins* (one) and *zwei* (two).

Money

Can you change dollars?	**Können Sie Dollar wechseln?**	**kurn**-nen zee **dol**-lar **vekh**-seln
What is your exchange rate for dollars...?	**Was ist ihr Wechselkurs für Dollars...?**	vahs ist eer **vekh**-sel-koors fewr **dol**-lars
...in traveler's checks	**...in Reiseschecks**	in **rī**-zeh-sheks
What is the commission?	**Wieviel ist die Kommission?**	vee-**feel** ist dee kom-mis-see-**ohn**
Any extra fee?	**Extra Gebühren?**	**ex**-trah geh-**bew**-ren
I would like...	**Ich hätte gern...**	ikh **het**-teh gehrn
...small bills.	**...kleine Banknoten.**	**klī**-neh **bahnk**-noh-ten
...large bills.	**...große Banknoten.**	**groh**-seh **bahnk**-noh-ten
...coins.	**...Münzen.**	**mewn**-tsen
...small change.	**...Kleingeld.**	**klīn**-gelt
Is this a mistake?	**Ist das ein Fehler?**	ist dahs īn **fay**-lehr
I'm...	**Ich bin...**	ikh bin
...broke / poor / rich.	**...pleite / arm / reich.**	**plī**-teh / arm / **rīkh**
55 DM	**fünfundfünfzig Mark**	**fewnf**-oont-**fewnf**-tsig mark
50 Pf	**fünfzig Pfennig**	**fewnf**-tsig **fehn**-nig

Key money words:

bank	**Bank**	bahnk
money	**Geld**	gelt
change money	**Geld wechseln**	gelt **vekh**-seln
exchange	**Wechsel**	**vekh**-sel
commission	**Kommission**	kom-mis-see-**ohn**
traveler's check	**Reisescheck**	rī-zeh-shek
credit card	**Kreditkarte**	kreh-**deet**-kar-teh
cash advance	**Vorschuß in Bargeld**	**for**-shoos in **bar**-gelt
cash machine	**Geldautomat**	gelt-ow-toh-**maht**
cashier	**Kassierer**	kah-**seer**-er
cash	**Bargeld**	**bar**-gelt
bills	**Banknoten**	**bahnk**-noh-ten
coins	**Münzen**	**mewn**-tsen
receipt	**Beleg**	bay-**leg**

German marks (DM) are divided into 100 pfennigs (Pf). Swiss francs (Fr) are divided into 100 centimes (c) or rappen (Rp). Use your common cents—pfennigs and centimes are like pennies, and each country has coins like nickels, dimes, and quarters. Austrian schillings are divided into 100 groschen, but since one schilling (1 AS) is worth about a dime, you'll rarely see coins less than a schilling.

Time

What time is it?	**Wie spät ist es?**	vee shpayt ist es
It's...	**Es ist...**	es ist
...8:00.	**...acht Uhr.**	ahkht oor
...16:00.	**...sechzehn Uhr.**	**zekh**-tsayn oor
...4:00 in the afternoon.	**...vier Uhr nachmittags.**	feer oor **nahkh**-mit-tahgs
...10:30 (half eleven) in the evening.	**...halb elf Uhr abends.**	hahlp elf oor **ah**-bents
...a quarter past nine.	**...viertel nach neun.**	**feer**-tel nahkh noyn
...a quarter to eleven.	**...viertel vor elf.**	**feer**-tel for elf
...noon.	**...Mittag.**	**mit**-tahg
...midnight.	**...Mitternacht.**	**mit**-ter-nahkht
...sunrise.	**...Sonnenaufgang.**	**zoh**-nen-owf-gahng
...sunset.	**...Sonnenuntergang.**	**zoh**-nen-oon-ter-gahng
...early / late.	**...früh / spät.**	frew / shpayt
...on time.	**...pünktlich.**	**pewnkt**-likh

In Germany, the 24-hour clock (or military time) is used by hotels, for the opening and closing hours of museums, and for train, bus, and boat schedules. Informally, the Germans use the same "12-hour clock" we use.

People use the greeting *"Guten Morgen"* (Good morning) until noon, and *"Guten Tag"* (Good day) switches to *"Guten Abend"* (Good evening) around 6 p.m.

Timely words:

minute	**Minute**	mee-**noo**-teh
hour	**Stunde**	**shtoon**-deh
morning	**Morgen**	**mor**-gen
afternoon	**Nachmittag**	**nahkh**-mit-tahg
evening	**Abend**	**ah**-bent
night	**Nacht**	nahkht
day	**Tag**	tahg
today	**heute**	**hoy**-teh
yesterday	**gestern**	**geh**-stern
tomorrow	**morgen**	**mor**-gen
tomorow morning	**morgen früh**	**mor**-gen frew
anytime	**jederzeit**	yay-der-**tsīt**
immediately	**jetzt**	yetst
in one hour	**in einer Stunde**	in ī-ner **shtoon**-deh
every hour	**jede Stunde**	**yay**-deh **shtoon**-deh
every day	**jeden Tag**	**yay**-den tahg
last	**letzte**	**lehts**-teh
this	**diese**	**dee**-zeh
next	**nächste**	**nekh**-steh
May 15	**fünfzehnten Mai**	**fewnf**-tsayn-ten mī

For dates of the month, take any number, add the sound "ten" to the end, then say the month. June 19 is *neunzehnten Juni.*

week	**Woche**	**vokh**-eh
Monday	**Montag**	**mohn**-tahg
Tuesday	**Dienstag**	**deen**-stahg
Wednesday	**Mittwoch**	**mit**-vokh
Thursday	**Donnerstag**	**don**-ner-stahg
Friday	**Freitag**	**frī**-tahg
Saturday	**Samstag, Sonnabend**	**zahm**-stahg, **zon**-ah-bent
Sunday	**Sonntag**	**zon**-tahg
month	**Monat**	**moh**-naht
January	**Januar**	**yah**-noo-ar
February	**Februar**	**fay**-broo-ar
March	**März**	mehrts
April	**April**	ah-**pril**
May	**Mai**	mī
June	**Juni**	**yoo**-nee
July	**Juli**	**yoo**-lee
August	**August**	ow-**gust**
September	**September**	sep-**tem**-ber
October	**Oktober**	ok-**toh**-ber
November	**November**	noh-**vem**-ber
December	**Dezember**	day-**tsem**-ber
year	**Jahr**	yar
spring	**Frühling**	**frew**-ling
summer	**Sommer**	**zom**-mer
fall	**Herbst**	hehrpst
winter	**Winter**	**vin**-ter

TIME

Happy days and holidays:

holiday	**Feiertag**	**fī**-er-tahg
national holiday	**staatlicher Feiertag**	**shtaht**-likh-er fī-er-tahg
religious holiday	**religiöser Feiertag**	reh-lig-ee-**ur**-zer fī-er-tahg
Easter	**Ostern**	**ohs**-tern
Merry Christmas!	**Fröhliche Weihnachten!**	**frur**-likh-en **vī**-nahkh-ten
Happy new year!	**Glückliches Neues Jahr!**	**glewk**-likh-es **noy**-es yar
Happy anniversary!	**Herzlichen Glückwunsch!**	**hehrts**-likh-en **glewk**-vunch
Happy birthday!	**Herzlichen Glückwunsch zum Geburtstag!**	**hehrts**-likh-en **glewk**-vunch tsoom geh-**boort**-stahg

The Germans sing "Happy birthday" to the same tune that we do, and even use the English words. Other German celebrations include *Karneval* (or *Fasching*), a week-long festival of parades and partying. It happens before Lent in February, and *Köln* is the center of the revelry. *Christi Himmelfahrt,* or the Ascension of Christ, comes in May, and doubles for Father's Day. You'll see men in groups on pilgrimages through the countryside, usually carrying beer or heading towards it.

Germany's national holiday is Oct. 3, Austria's is Oct. 26, and Switzerland's is Aug. 1.

Transportation

TRANSPORTATION

Trains:

Is this the line for...?	**Ist das die Schlange für...?**	ist dahs dee **shlahn**-geh fewr
...tickets	**...Fahrkarten**	**far**-kar-ten
...reservations	**...Reservierungen**	reh-zehr-**vee**-roong-en
How much is a ticket to...?	**Wieviel kostet eine Fahrkarte nach...?**	voo feel **kos**-tet **ī**-neh **far**-kar-teh nahkh
A ticket to ___.	**Eine Fahrkarte nach ___.**	**ī**-neh **far**-kar-teh nahkh
When is the next train?	**Wann ist der nächste Zug?**	vahn ist dehr **nekh**-steh tsoog
I'd like to leave...	**Ich möchte... abfahren.**	ikh **murkh**-teh... **ahp**-fah-ren
I'd like to arrive...	**Ich möchte... ankommen.**	ikh **murkh**-teh... **ahn**-kom-men
...by ___.	**...vor ___**	for
...in the morning.	**...am Morgen**	ahm **mor**-gen
...in the afternoon.	**...am Nachmittag**	ahm **nahkh**-mit-tahg
...in the evening.	**...am Abend**	ahm **ah**-bent

Is there a...?	Gibt es einen...?	gipt es ī-nen
...earlier train	...früherer Zug	**frew**-hehr-er tsoog
...later train	...späterer Zug	**shpay**-ter-er tsoog
...overnight train	...Nachtzug	**nahkht**-tsoog
...supplement	...Zuschlag	**tsoo**-shlahg
Is there a discount for...?	Gibt es Ermäßigung für...?	gipt es ehr-**may**-see-goong fewr
...youths	...Jugendliche	yoo-gend-**likh**-eh
...seniors	...Senioren	zen-**yor**-en
Is a reservation required?	Brauche ich eine Platzkarte?	**browkh**-eh ikh ī-neh **plahts**-kar-teh
I'd like to reserve a...	Ich möchte einen... reservieren.	ikh **murkh**-teh ī-nen... reh-zer-**vee**-ren
...seat.	...Sitzplatz	**zits**-plahts
...berth.	...Liegewagenplatz	**lee**-geh-vah-gen-plahts
...sleeper.	...Schlafwagenplatz	**shlahf**-vah-gen-plahts
Where does (the train) leave from?	Von wo geht er ab?	fon voh gayt ehr ahp
What track?	Welchem Gleis?	**velkh**-em glīs
On time? Late?	Pünktlich? Spät?	**pewnkt**-likh / shpayt
When will it arrive?	Wann kommt er an?	vahn komt ehr ahn
Is it direct?	Direktverbindung?	dee-**rekt**-fehr-bin-doong
Must I transfer?	Muß ich umsteigen?	mus ikh **oom**-shtī-gen
When? Where?	Wann? Wo?	vahn / voh
Which train to...?	Welcher Zug nach...?	**velkh**-er tsoog nahkh
Which train car to...?	Welcher Wagen nach...?	**velkh**-er **vah**-gen nahkh

Is this seat free?	**Ist dieser Platz frei?**	ist **dee**-zer plahts frī
That's my seat.	**Das ist mein Platz.**	dahs ist mīn plahts
Save my place?	**Halten Sie meinen Platz frei?**	**halh**-ten zee **mī**-nen plahts frī
Where are you going?	**Wohin fahren Sie?**	**voh**-hin **far**-en zee
I'm going to...	**Ich fahre nach...**	ikh **far**-reh nahk
Can you tell me when to get off?	**Können Sie mir Bescheid sagen?**	**kurn**-nen zee meer beh-**shīt** zah-gen

TRANSPORTATION

Ticket talk:

ticket	**Fahrkarte**	**far**-kar-teh
one-way ticket	**Hinfahrkarte**	**hin**-far-kar-teh
roundtrip ticket	**Rückfahrkarte**	**rewk**-far-kar-teh
first class	**erster Klasse**	**ehr**-ster **klah**-seh
second class	**zweiter Klasse**	**tsvī**-ter **klah**-seh
reduced fare	**verbilligte Karte**	fehr-**bil**-lig-teh **kar**-teh
validate	**abstempeln**	**ahp**-shtem-peln
schedule	**Fahrplan**	**far**-plahn
departure	**Abfahrtszeit**	**ahp**-farts-tsīt
direct	**Direkt**	dee-**rekt**
connection	**Anschluß**	**ahn**-shlus
reservation	**Platzkarte**	**plahts**-kar-teh
non-smoking	**Nichtraucher**	**nikht**-rowkh-er
seat	**Platz**	plahts
window seat	**Fensterplatz**	**fen**-ster-plahts
aisle seat	**Platz am Gang**	plahts ahm gahng

berth...	**Liege...**	**lee**-geh
...upper	**...obere**	**oh**-ber-eh
...middle	**...mittlere**	mit-**leh**-reh
...lower	**...untere**	**oon**-ter-eh
refund	**Rückvergütung**	**rewk**-fehr-gew-toong

At the train station:

German State Railways	**Deutsche Bundes-bahn (DB)**	**doy**-cheh **boon**-des-bahn (day bay)
train station	**Bahnhof**	**bahn**-hohf
central train station	**Hauptbahnhof**	**howpt**-bahn-hohf
train information	**Zugauskunft**	tsoog-**ows**-koonft
train	**Zug, Eisenbahn**	tsoog, **ī**-zen-bahn
high speed train	**Intercity, Schnellzug**	"inter-city," **shnel**-tsoog
arrival	**Ankunft**	**ahn**-koonft
departure	**Abfahrt**	**ahp**-fart
delay	**Verspätung**	fehr-**shpay**-toong
waiting room	**Wartesaal**	**var**-teh-zahl
lockers	**Schließfächer**	**shlees**-fekh-er
baggage check room	**Gepäckaufgabe**	geh-**pek**-owf-**gah**-beh
lost and found office	**Fundbüro**	**foond**-bew-roh
tourist information	**Touristen-information**	**too**-ris-ten-in-for-maht-see-**ohn**
to the trains	**zu den Zugen**	tsoo dayn **tsoo**-gen
platform	**Bahnsteig**	**bahn**-shtīg
track	**Gleis**	glīs

train car	**Wagen**	**vah**-gen
dining car	**Speisewagen**	**shpī**-zeh-vah-gen
sleeper car	**Liegewagen**	**lee**-geh-vah-gen
conductor	**Schaffner**	**shahf**-ner

TRANSPORTATION

Reading train schedules:

Abfahrt	departure
Ankunft	arrival
außer	except
bis	until
Feiertag	holiday
jeden	every
nach	to
nur	only
Richtung	direction
Samstag	Saturday
Sonntag	Sunday
täglich (tgl.)	daily
tagsüber	days
über	via
verspätet	late
von	from
werktags	Monday-Saturday (workdays)
wochentags	weekdays
1-5, 6, 7	Monday-Friday, Saturday, Sunday

German schedules use the 24-hour clock. It's like American time until noon. After that, subtract twelve and add p.m. So 13:00 is 1 p.m., 20:00 is 8 p.m., and 24:00 is midnight. One minute after midnight is 00:01.

Major rail lines in Germany, Austria, and Switzerland

Buses and subways:

How do I get to...?	**Wie komme ich zu...?**	vee **kom**-meh ikh tsoo
Which bus to...?	**Welcher Bus nach...?**	**velkh**-er boos nahkh
Does it stop at...?	**Hält er in...?**	helt er in
Which stop for...?	**Welche Haltestelle für...?**	**velkh**-eh **hahl**-teh-shtel-leh fewr
Must I transfer?	**Muß ich umsteigen?**	mus ikh **oom**-shtī-gen
How much is a ticket?	**Wieviel kostet eine Fahrkarte?**	vee-**feel kos**-tet ī-neh **far**-kar-teh
Where can I buy a ticket?	**Wo kaufe ich eine Fahrkarte?**	voh **kow**-feh ikh ī-neh **far**-kar-teh
Is there a...?	**Gibt es eine...?**	gipt es ī-neh
...one-day pass	**...Tagesnetzkarte**	**tahg**-es-nets kar teh
...discount for buying more tickets	**...Preisnachlaß, wenn ich mehrere Fahrkarten kaufe?**	prīs-**nahkh**-lahs ven ikh **meh**-reh-reh **far**-kar-ten **kow**-feh
When is the...?	**Wann fährt der... ab?**	vahn fart dehr... ahp
...first	**...erste**	**ehr**-steh
...next	**...nächste**	**nekh**-steh
...last	**...letzte**	**lets**-teh
...bus / subway	**...Bus / U-Bahn**	boos / **oo**-bahn
What's the frequency per hour / day?	**Wie oft pro Stunde / Tag?**	vee oft proh **shtoon**-deh / tahg
I'm going to...	**Ich fahre nach...**	ikh **far**-eh nahkh
Can you tell me when to get off?	**Können Sie mir Bescheid sagen?**	**kurn**-nen zee meer beh-**shīt** zah-gen

TRANSPORTATION

Key bus & subway words:

ticket	**Fahrkarte**	**far**-kar-teh
bus	**Bus**	boos
bus stop	**Bushaltestelle**	**boos**-hahl-teh-**shtel**-leh
bus station	**Busbahnhof**	**boos**-bahn-hof
subway	**U-Bahn**	**oo**-bahn
subway map	**U-Bahnkarte**	**oo**-bahn-kar-teh
subway entrance	**U-Bahnstation**	**oo**-bahn-shtaht-see-ohn
subway stop	**U-Bahnhaltestelle**	**oo**-bahn-hahl-teh-**shtel**-leh
subway exit	**U-Bahnausgang**	**oo**-bahn-ows-gahng
direct	**Direkt**	dee-**rekt**
direction	**Richtung**	**rikh**-toong
connection	**Anschluß**	**ahn**-shlus

Most big cities offer deals on transportation, such as one-day tickets, cheaper fares for youths and seniors, or a discount for buying a batch of tickets (which you can share with friends). Major cities in Germany, such as Munich and Berlin, have a *U-Bahn* (subway) and *S-Bahn* (urban rail system). If your Eurailpass is valid on the day you're traveling, you can use the *S-Bahn* for free.

Taxis:

Taxi!	**Taxi!**	**tahk**-see
Can you call a taxi?	**Können Sie mir ein Taxi rufen?**	**kurn**-nen zee meer īn **tahk**-see **roo**-fen
Where is a taxi stand?	**Wo ist ein Taxistand?**	voh ist īn **tahk**-see-shtahnt
Are you free?	**Sind Sie frei?**	zint zee frī
Occupied.	**Besetzt.**	beh-**zetst**
How much will it cost to...?	**Wieviel kostet die Fahrt...?**	vee-**feel kos**-tet dee fart
...the airport	**...zum Flughafen**	zoom **floog**-hah-fen
...the train station	**...zum Bahnhof**	zoom **bahn**-hof
...this address	**...zu dieser Adresse**	zoo **dee**-zer ah-**dres**-seh
Too much.	**Zu viel.**	tsoo feel
This is all I have.	**Mehr habe ich nicht.**	mehr **hah**-beh ikh nikht
Can you take ___ people?	**Können Sie ___ Personen mitnehman?**	**kurn**-nen zee ___ pehr-**zoh**-nen mit-**nay**-mahn
Any extra fee?	**Extra Gebühren?**	ex-trah geh-**bew**-ren
The meter, please.	**Den Zähler, bitte.**	dayn **tsay**-ler **bit**-teh
The most direct route.	**Auf direktem Weg.**	owf dee-**rek**-tem vayg
Slow down.	**Fahren Sie langsamer.**	far on zee **lahng**-zah-mer
If you don't slow down, I'll throw up.	**Wenn Sie nicht langsamer fahren, wird mir schlecht.**	ven zee nikht **lahng**-zah-mer **far**-en virt meer shlekht
Stop here.	**Halten Sie hier.**	**hahl** tcn zee heer

Can you wait?	Können Sie warten?	**kurn**-nen zee **var**-ten
I'll never forget this ride.	**Diese Fahrt werde ich nie vergessen.**	**dee**-zeh fart **vehr**-deh ikh nee fehr-**geh**-sen
Where did you learn to drive?	**Wo haben Sie Autofahren gelernt?**	voh **hah**-ben zee **ow**-toh-far-en geh-**lehrnt**
I'll only pay what's on the meter.	**Ich bezahle nur, was auf dem Zähler steht.**	ikh beht-**sah**-leh noor vahs owf daym **tsay**-ler shtayt
My change, please.	**Mein Wechselgeld, bitte.**	mīn **vek**-sel-gelt **bit**-teh
Keep the change.	**Stimmt so.**	shtimt zoh

Ride in style in a German taxi—usually a BMW or Mercedes. If you're having a tough time hailing a taxi, ask for the nearest taxi stand. The German word: *Taxistand*. Tipping isn't expected, but it's polite to round up. So if the fare is 19 marks, round up to 20.

Rental wheels:

I'd like to rent a...	**Ich möchte ein...** **mieten.**	ikh **murkh**-teh īn... **mee**-ten
...car.	**...Auto**	**ow**-toh
...station wagon.	**...Kombi**	**kohm**-bee
...van.	**...Kleinbus**	**klīn**-boos
...motorcycle.	**...Motorrad**	**moh**-tor-raht
...motor scooter.	**...Moped**	**moh**-ped
...bicycle.	**...Fahrrad**	**far**-raht
...tank.	**...Pahnzer**	**pahn**-tser
How much per...?	**Wieviel pro...?**	vee-**feel** proh
...hour	**...Stunde**	**shtoon**-deh
...day	**...Tag**	tahg
...week	**...Woche**	**vokh**-eh
Unlimited mileage?	**Unbegrenzte kilometer?**	oon-beh-**grents**-teh kee-loh-**may**-ter
I brake for bakeries.	**Ich bremse für Bäckereien.**	ikh **brem**-zeh fewr bek-eh-**rī**-en
Is there a...?	**Gibt es eine...?**	gipt es **ī**-neh
...helmet	**...Helm**	helm
...discount	**...Ermäßigung**	ehr-**may**-see-goong
...deposit	**...Kaution**	**kowt**-see-ohn
...insurance	**...Versicherung**	fehr-**zikh**-eh-roong
When do I bring it back?	**Wann bringe ich es zurück?**	vahn **bring**-geh ikh es tsoo-**rewk**

Driving:

gas station	**Tankstelle**	**tahnk**-shtel-leh
The nearest gas station?	**Die nächste Tankstelle?**	dee **nekh**-steh **tahnk**-shtel-leh
Self-service?	**Selbstbedienung?**	**zehlpst**-beh-dee-noong
Fill the tank.	**Volltanken.**	**fol**-tahnk-en
I need...	**Ich brauche...**	ikh **browkh**-eh
...gas.	**...Benzin.**	ben-**tseen**
...unleaded.	**...Bleifrei.**	**blī**-frī
...regular.	**...Normal.**	nor-**mahl**
...super.	**...Super.**	**zoo**-per
...diesel.	**...Diesel.**	**dee**-zel
Check the...	**Sehen Sie nach...**	**zay**-hen zee nahkh
...oil.	**...Öl.**	url
...air in the tires.	**...Luftdruck in Reifen.**	**luft**-druk in **rī**-fen
...radiator.	**...Kühler.**	**kew**-ler
...battery.	**...Batterie.**	baht-teh-**ree**
...fuses.	**...Sicherungen.**	**zikh**-eh-roong-en
...fanbelt.	**...Keilriemen.**	**kīl**-ree-men
...brakes.	**...Bremsen.**	**brem**-zen
...my pulse.	**...Puls.**	pools

Getting gas is a piece of *Strudel*. Regular is *normal* and super is *super*, and marks and liters replace dollars and gallons. If a mark is 2/3 of a dollar and there are about 4 liters in a gallon, gas costing 1.50 DM a liter = $4 a gallon.

Car trouble:

accident	**Unfall**	**oon**-fahl
breakdown	**Panne**	**pah**-neh
funny noise	**komisches Geräusch**	**koh**-mish-es geh-**roysh**
electrical problem	**elektrische Schwierigkeiten**	eh-**lek**-trish-eh **shvee**-rig-kī-ten
flat tire	**Reifenpanne**	**rī**-fen-pah-neh
My car won't start.	**Mein Auto springt nicht an.**	mīn **ow**-toh shpringt nikht ahn
This doesn't work.	**Das geht nicht.**	dahs gayt nikht
It's overheating.	**Es überhitzt.**	es **ew**-behr-hitst
My car is broken.	**Mein Auto ist kaputt.**	mīn **ow**-toh ist kah-**put**
I need a...	**Ich brauche einen...**	ikh **browkh**-eh ī-nen
...tow truck.	**...Abschleppwagen.**	**ahp**-shlep-vah-gen
...mechanic.	**...Mechaniker.**	mekh-**ahn**-i-ker
...stiff drink.	**...Schnaps.**	shnahps

For help with repair, look up "Repair" under Shopping.

Parking:

parking garage	**Garage**	gah-**rah**-zhoh
Where can I park?	**Wo kann ich parken?**	voh kahn ikh **par**-ken
Is parking nearby?	**Gibt es Parkplätze in der Nähe?**	gipt es **park**-plet-seh in dehr **nay**-heh
Can I park here?	**Darf ich hier parken?**	darf ikh heer **par**-ken

How long can I park here?	**Wie lange darf ich hier parken?**	vee **lahng**-eh darf ikh heer **par**-ken
Must I pay to park here?	**Kostet Parken hier etwas?**	**kos**-tet **par**-ken heer **et**-vahs
Is this a safe place to park?	**Ist dies ein sicherer Parkplatz?**	ist deez īn **zikh**-her-er **park**-plahts

Finding your way:

I'm going to... (if you're on foot)	**Ich gehe nach...**	ikh **gay**-heh nahkh
I'm going to... (if you're using wheels)	**Ich fahre nach...**	ikh **fah**-reh nahkh
How do I get to...?	**Wie komme ich nach...?**	vee **kom**-meh ikh nahkh
Do you have a...?	**Haben Sie eine...?**	**hah**-ben zee ī-neh
...city map	**...Stadtplan**	**shtaht**-plahn
...road map	**...Straßenkarte**	**shtrah**-sen-kar-teh
How many minutes / hours...?	**Wieviele Minuten / Stunden...?**	vee-**fee**-leh mee-**noo**-ten / **shtoon**-den
...by foot	**...zu Fuß**	tsoo foos
...by bicycle	**...mit dem Rad**	mit daym raht
...by car	**...mit dem Auto**	mit daym **ow**-toh
How many kilometers to...?	**Wieviele Kilometer sind es nach...?**	vee-**fee**-leh kee-loh-**may**-ter zint es nahkh
What's the...	**Was ist der...**	vahs ist dehr...
route to Berlin?	**Weg nach Berlin?**	vayg nahkh behr-**lin**
...best	**...beste**	**bes**-teh

...fastest	**...schnellste**	**shnel**-steh
...most interesting	**...interessanteste**	in-tehr-es-**sahn**-tes-teh
Point it out?	**Zeigen Sie es mir?**	**tsī**-gen zee es meer
I'm lost.	**Ich habe mich verlaufen.**	ikh **hah**-beh mikh fehr-**lowf**-en
Where am I?	**Wo bin ich?**	voh bin ikh
Who am I?	**Wie heiße ich?**	vee **hī**-seh ikh
Where is...?	**Wo ist...?**	voh ist
The nearest...?	**Der nächste...?**	dehr **nekh**-steh
Where is this address?	**Wo ist diese Adresse?**	voh ist **dee**-zeh ah-**dres**-seh

TRANSPORTATION

Key route-finding words:

city map	**Stadtplan**	**shtaht**-plahn
road map	**Straßenkarte**	**shtrah**-sen-kar-teh
straight ahead	**geradeaus**	geh-**rah**-deh-**ows**
left / right	**links / rechts**	links / rekhts
first / next	**erste / nächste**	**ehr**-steh / **nekh**-steh
intersection	**Kreuzung**	**kroy**-tsoong
stoplight	**Ampel**	**ahm**-pel
(main) square	**(Markt)platz**	**(markt)**-plahts
street	**Straße**	**shtrah**-seh
bridge	**Brücke**	**brew**-keh
tunnel	**Tunnel**	**too**-nel
highway	**Landstraße**	**lahnd**-shtrah-seh
freeway	**Autobahn**	**ow**-toh-bahn
north / south	**Norden / Süden**	**nor**-den / **zew**-den
east / west	**Osten / Westen**	**os**-ten / **ves**-ten

Reading German road signs:

Alle Richtungen	out of town (all destinations)
Ausfahrt	exit
Autobahn Kreuz	freeway interchange
Dreieck	"3-corner" or fork
Einbahnstrasse	one-way street
Einfahrt	entrance
Fussgänger	pedestrians
Gebühr	toll
Langsam	slow down
Parken verboten	no parking
Stadtmitte	to the center of town
Stopp	stop
Strassen-arbeiten	road workers ahead
Umleitung	detour
Vorfahrt beachten	yield
Zentrum	to the center of town

Here are the standard symbols you'll see:

STOP   No Entry For Cars   All Vehicles Prohibited   No Entry   Speed Limit (in km)   Yield   No Passing   Danger   Parking

The shortest distance between any two points in Germany is the *Autobahn*. The right to no speed limit is as close to the average German driver's heart as the right to bear arms is to many American hearts. To survive, never cruise in the passing lane. While all roads seem to lead to the little town of *Ausfahrt*, that is the German word for exit. The *Autobahn* information magazine, available at any *Autobahn Tankstelle* (gas station), lists all road signs, interchanges, and the hours and facilities available at various rest stops. Missing a turnoff can cost you lots of time and miles—be alert for *Autobahn Kreuz* (interchange) signs.

As in any country, the flashing lights of a patrol car are a sure sign that someone's in trouble. If it's you, try this handy phrase: *"Entschuldigung, ich bin Tourist"* (Sorry, I'm a tourist). Or, for the adventurous: *"Wenn Ihnen nicht gefält, wie ich Auto fahre, gehen Sie doch vom Gehweg runter."* (If you don't like how I drive, stay off the sidewalk.)

The German word for journey or trip is *Fahrt*. Many tourists enjoy collecting Fahrts. In Germany you'll see signs for *Einfahrt* (entrance), *Rundfahrt* (round trip), *Rückfahrt* (return trip), *Himmelfahrt* (ascend to heaven day, August 15th), *Panoramafahrt* (scenic journey), *Zugfahrt* (train trip), *Ausfahrt* (trip out), and throughout your trip, people will smile and wish you a *"Gute Fahrt."*

TRANSPORTATION

Other signs you may bump into:

belegt	no vacancy
besetzt	occupied
Damen	women
Eintritt frei	free admission
Gefahr	danger
geöffnet von... bis...	open from... to...
geöffnet	open
geschlossen	closed
Herren	men
kein Eingang, keine Einfahrt	no entry
kein Trinkwasser	undrinkable water
lebensgefährlich	extremely dangerous
nicht rauchen	no smoking
Notausgang	emergency exit
Ruhetag	closed (quiet day)
Stammtisch	reserved table for regulars
Toiletten	toilet
Verboten	forbidden
Vorsicht	caution
WC	toilet
wegen Umbau geschlossen	closed for restoration
wegen Ferien geschlossen	closed for vacation
Zimmer frei	vacancy
zu verkaufen	for sale
zu vermieten	for rent or for hire
Zugang verboten	keep out

Sleeping

Places to stay:

hotel	**Hotel**	hoh-**tel**
small hotel	**Pension**	pen-see-**ohn**
room in a home or bed & breakfast	**Gästezimmer, Fremdenzimmer**	**ges**-teh-tsim-mer, **frem**-den-tsim-mer
youth hostel	**Jugendherberge**	**yoo**-gend-hehr-behr-geh
vacancy	**Zimmer frei**	**tsim**-mer frī
no vacancy	**belegt**	beh-**legt**

SLEEPING

Reserving a room:

If you reserve a room by phone, a good time to call is the morning of the day you plan to arrive. To reserve by fax, use the nifty form in the appendix.

Hello.	**Gutentag.**	**goo**-ten tahg
My name is...	**Ich heiße...**	ikh **hī**-seh
Do you speak English?	**Sprechen Sie Englisch?**	**shprekh**-en zee **eng**-lish
Do you have a room...?	**Haben Sie ein Zimmer...?**	**hah**-ben zee īn **tsim**-mer
...for one person	**...für eine Person**	fewr **ī**-neh pehr-**zohn**
...for two people	**...für zwei Personen**	fewr tsvī pehr-**zoh**-nen
...for tonight	**...für heute abend**	fewr **hoy**-teh **ah**-bent
...for two nights	**...für zwei Nächte**	fewr tsvī **naykh**-teh
...for Friday	**...für Freitag**	fewr **frī**-tahg

...for June 21	...für einund- zwanzigsten Juni	fewr **īn**-oont- tsvahn-tsig-ten **yoo**-nee
Yes or no?	**Ja oder nein?**	yah **oh**-der nīn
I'd like...	**Ich möchte...**	ikh **murkh**-teh
...a private bathroom.	**...eigenes Bad.**	**ī**-geh-nes baht
...your cheapest room.	**...ihr billigstes Zimmer.**	eer **bil**-lig-stes **tsim**-mer
...___ bed(s) for ___ people in ___ room(s).	**...___ Bett(en) für ___ Personen in ___ Zimmer(n).**	___ bet-(ten) fewr ___ pehr-**zoh**-nen in ___ **tsim**-mer(n)
How much is it?	**Wieviel kostet das?**	vee-**feel kos**-tet dahs
Anything cheaper?	**Etwas billigeres?**	**et**-vahs **bil**-lig-er-es
I'll take it.	**Ich nehme es.**	ikh **nay**-meh es
I'll stay for...	**Ich bleibe für...**	ikh **blī**-beh fewr
We'll stay for...	**Wir bleiben für...**	veer **blī**-ben fewr
...one night.	**...eine nacht.**	**ī**-neh nahkht
...___ nights.	**...___ nächte.**	___ **naykh**-teh
I'll come...	**Ich komme...**	ikh **kom**-meh
We'll come...	**Wir kommen...**	veer **kom**-men
...in one hour.	**...in einer Stunde.**	in **ī**-ner **shtoon**-deh
...before 16:00.	**...vor sechzehn Uhr.**	for **zekh**-tsayn oor
...Friday before 6 p.m.	**...Freitag vor sechs Uhr abends.**	**frī**-tahg for zex oor **ah**-bents
Thank you.	**Danke.**	**dahng**-keh

Getting specific:

I'd like a room...	**Ich möchte ein Zimmer...**	ikh **murkh**-teh īn **tsim**-mer
...with / without / and	**...mit / ohne / und**	mit / **oh**-neh / oont
...toilet	**...Toilette**	toh-**leh**-teh
...shower	**...Dusche**	**doo**-sheh
...shower down the hall	**...Dusche im Gang**	**doo**-sheh im gahng
...bathtub	**...Badewanne**	**bah**-deh-vah-neh
...double bed	**...Doppelbett**	**dop**-pel-bet
...twin beds	**...zwei Einzelbetten**	tsvī īn-tsel-bet-ten
...balcony	**...Balkon**	**bahl**-kohn
...view	**...Ausblick**	**ows**-blick
...with only a sink	**...nur mit Waschbecken**	noor mit **vahsh**-bek-en
...on the ground floor	**...im Erdgeschoß**	im **ehrd**-geh-shos
Is there an elevator?	**Gibt es einen Fahrstuhl?**	gipt es ī-nen **far**-shtool
We arrive Monday, depart Wednesday.	**Wir kommen am Montag, und reisen am Mittwoch ab.**	veer **kom**-men ahm **mohn**-tahg oont rī-zen ahm **mit**-vokh ahp
I have a reservation.	**Ich habe eine Reservierung.**	ikh **hah**-beh ī-neh reh-zehr-**vee**-roong
Confirm my reservation?	**Meine Reservierung bestätigen?**	**mī**-neh reh-zehr-**vee**-roong beh-**shtet**-i-gen

SLEEPING

| I'll sleep anywhere. I'm desperate. | **Ich kann auf dem Fußboden schlafen. Ich bin am Verzweifeln.** | ikh kahn owf daym **foos**-boh-den **shlah**-fen. ikh bin ahm fehr-**tsvī**-feln |
| I have a sleeping bag. | **Ich habe einen Schlafsack.** | ikh **hah**-beh **ī**-nen **shlahf**-zahk |

Nailing down the price:

How much is...?	**Wieviel kostet...?**	vee-**feel kos**-tet
...a room for ___ people	**...ein Zimmer für ___ Personen**	īn tsim-mer fewr ___ pehr-**zoh**-nen
...your cheapest room	**...ihr billigstes Zimmer**	eer **bil**-lig-stes **tsim**-mer
Breakfast included?	**Frühstück eingeschlossen?**	**frew**-shtewk **īn**-geh-shlos-sen
Is breakfast required?	**Ist Frühstück Bedingung?**	ist **frew**-shtewk beh-**ding**-oong
How much without breakfast?	**Wieviel ohne Frühstück?**	vee-**feel oh**-neh **frew**-shtewk
Complete price?	**Vollpreis?**	**fol**-prīs
Is it cheaper if I stay ___ nights?	**Ist is billiger, wenn ich ___ Nächte bleibe?**	ist es **bil**-lig-er ven ikh ___ **naykh**-teh **blī**-beh
I'll stay ___ nights.	**Ich werde ___ Nächte bleiben.**	ikh **vehr**-deh ___ **naykh**-teh **blī**-ben

Choosing a room:

Can I see the room?	**Kann ich das Zimmer sehen?**	kahn ikh dahs **tsim**-mer **zay**-hen
Show me another room?	**Zeigen Sie mir ein anderes Zimmer?**	**tsī**-gen zee meer īn **ahn**-der-es **tsim**-mer
Do you have something...?	**Haben Sie etwas...?**	**hah**-ben zee **et**-vahs
...larger / smaller	**...größeres / kleineres**	**grur**-ser-es / **klī**-ner-es
...better / cheaper	**...besseres / billigeres**	**bes**-ser-es / **bil**-lig-er-es
...brighter	**...heller**	**hel**-ler
...in the back	**...nach hinten hinaus**	nahkh **hin**-ten hin-**ows**
...quieter	**...ruhigeres**	**roo**-i-ger-es
I'll take it.	**Ich nehme es.**	ikh **nay**-meh es
My key.	**Meinen Schlüssel.**	**mī**-nen **shlew**-sel
Sleep well.	**Schlafen Sie gut.**	**shlah**-fen zee goot
Good night.	**Gute Nacht.**	**goo**-teh nahkht

Hotel help:

I'd like...	**Ich hätte gern...**	ikh **het**-teh gehrn
...a / another	**...ein / noch ein**	īn / nokh īn
...towel.	**...Handtuch.**	**hahnd**-tookh
...pillow.	**...Kissen.**	**kis**-sen
...clean sheets.	**...saubere Laken.**	**zow**-ber-eh **lah**-ken
...blanket.	**...Decke.**	**dek**-eh
...glass.	**...Glas.**	glahs

SLEEPING

...sink stopper.	**...Abflußstöpsel.**	**ahp**-floos-shtohp-zel
...soap.	**...Seife.**	**zī**-feh
...toilet paper.	**...Klopapier.**	**kloh**-pah-peer
...crib.	**...Kinderbett.**	**kin**-der-bet
...small extra bed.	**...kleines Extrabett.**	**klī**-nes **ehk**-strah-bet
...different room.	**...anderes Zimmer.**	**ahn**-der-es **tsim**-mer
...silence.	**...Ruhe.**	**roo**-heh
Where can I wash / hang my laundry?	**Wo kann ich meine Wäsche waschen / aufhängen?**	voh kahn ikh **mī**-neh **vesh**-eh **vahsh**-en / **owf**-heng-en
I'd like to stay another night.	**Ich möchte noch eine Nacht bleiben.**	ikh **murkh**-teh nokh **ī**-neh nahkht **blī**-ben
Where can I park?	**Wo soll ich parken?**	voh zol ikh **par**-ken
What time do you lock up?	**Um wieviel Uhr schließen Sie ab?**	oom vee-**feel** oor **shlee**-sen zee ahp
What time is breakfast?	**Um wieviel Uhr ist Frühstück?**	oom vee-**feel** oor ist **frew**-shtewk
Please wake me at 7:00.	**Wecken Sie mich um sieben Uhr, bitte.**	**vek**-en zee mikh oom **zee**-ben oor **bit**-teh

Hotel hassles:

Come with me.	**Kommen Sie mit.**	**kom**-men zee mit
I have a problem in my room.	**Es gibt ein Problem mit meinem Zimmer.**	es gipt īn proh-**blaym** mit **mī**-nem **tsim**-mer
It smells bad.	**Es stinkt.**	es shtinkt
bugs	**Wanzen**	**vahn**-tsen

mice	**Mäuse**	**moy**-zeh
prostitutes	**Freudenmädchen**	**froy**-den-mayd-khen
The bed is too soft / hard.	**Das Bett ist zu weich / hart.**	dahs bet ist tsoo vīkh / hart
I'm covered with bug bites.	**Ich bin mit Wanzenbissen übersäht.**	ikh bin mit **vahn**-tsen-**bis**-sen ew-ber-**zayt**
Lamp...	**Lampe...**	**lahm**-peh
Lightbulb...	**Birne...**	**bir**-neh
Key...	**Schlüssel...**	**shlew**-sel
Lock...	**Schloß...**	shlos
Window...	**Fenster...**	**fen**-ster
Faucet...	**Wasserhahn...**	**vah**-ser-hahn
Sink...	**Waschbecken...**	**vahsh**-bek-en
Toilet...	**Klo...**	kloh
Shower...	**Dusche...**	**doo**-sheh
...doesn't work.	**...ist kaputt.**	ist kah-**put**
There is no hot water.	**Es gibt kein warmes Wasser.**	es gipt kīn **var**-mes **vahs**-ser
When is the water hot?	**Wann wird das Wasser warm?**	vahn virt dahs **vahs**-ser varm

Checking out:

I'll leave...	**Ich fahre... ab.**	ikh **fah**-reh... ahp
We'll leave...	**Wir fahren... ab.**	veer **fah**-ren... ahp
...today / tomorrow	**...heute / morgen**	**hoy**-teh / **mor**-gen
...very early	**...sehr früh**	zehr frew

SLEEPING

When is check-out time?	**Wann muß ich das Zimmer verlassen?**	vahn mus ikh dahs **tsim**-mer fehr-**lah**-sen
Can I pay now?	**Kann ich zahlen?**	kahn ikh **tsah**-len
Bill, please.	**Rechnung, bitte.**	**rekh**-noong **bit**-teh
Credit card O.K.?	**Kreditkarte O.K.?**	kreh-**deet**-kar-teh "O.K."
I slept like a bear.	**Ich habe wie ein Bär geschlafen.**	ikh **hah**-beh vee īn bar geh-**shlahf**-en
Everything was great.	**Alles war gut.**	**ahl**-les var goot
Will you call my next hotel for me?	**Können Sie mein nächstes Hotel anrufen?**	**kurn**-nen zee mīn **nekh**-stes hoh-**tel** **ahn**-roo-fen
Can I...?	**Kann ich...?**	kahn ikh
Can we...?	**Können wir...?**	**kurn**-nen veer
...leave luggage here until ___	**...das Gepäck hierlassen bis ___**	dahs geh-**pek** **heer**-lah-sen bis

Camping:

tent	**Zelt**	tselt
camping	**Camping**	**kahm**-ping
Where is a campground?	**Wo ist ein Campingplatz?**	voh ist īn **kahm**-ping-plahts
Can I...?	**Kann ich...?**	kahn ikh
Can we...?	**Können wir...?**	**kurn**-nen veer
...camp here for one night	**...hier eine Nacht zelten**	heer ī-neh nahkht **tsehl**-ten
Are showers included?	**Duschen eingeschlossen?**	**doo**-shen **īn**-geh-shlos-sen

Eating

EATING

Finding a restaurant:

Where's a good... restaurant nearby?	**Wo ist hier ein gutes... Restaurant?**	voh ist heer īn **goo**-tes... res-tow-**rahnt**
...cheap	**...billiges**	**bil**-lig-es
...local-style	**...typisches**	**tew**-pish-es
...untouristy	**...nicht für Touristen gedachtes**	nikht fewr too-**ris**-ten geh-**dahkh**-tes
...Chinese	**...chinesisches**	khee-**nayz**-ish-es
...Italian	**...italienisches**	i-**tahl**-yehn-ish-es
...Turkish	**...türkisches**	**tewrk**-ish-es
...fast food	**...Schnellimbiß**	shnel-**im**-bis
...self-service buffet	**...Selbstbedienungsbuffett**	**zelpst**-beh-dee-noongs-boo-fay
with a salad bar	**mit Salatbar**	mit zah-**laht**-bar

Getting a table and menu:

Waiter.	**Kellner.**	**kel**-ner
Waitress.	**Kellnerin.**	**kel**-ner-in
I'd like...	**Ich hätte gern...**	ikh **het**-teh gehrn
...a table for one / two.	**...einen Tisch für ein / zwei.**	**ī**-nen tish fewr īn / tsvī
...non-smoking.	**...Nichtraucher.**	**nikht**-rowkh-er
...just a drink.	**...nur etwas zu trinken.**	noor **et**-vahs tsoo **trink**-en
...a snack.	**...eine Kleinigkeit.**	**ī**-neh **klī**-nig-kīt

Can I...?	**Kann ich...?**	kahn ikh
...see the menu	**...die Karte sehen**	dee **kar**-teh **zay**-hen
...order	**...bestellen**	beh-**shtel**-len
...pay	**...zahlen**	**tsahl**-en
...throw up	**...mich übergeben**	mikh **ew**-ber-gay-ben
What do you recommend?	**Was schlagen Sie vor?**	vahs **shlah**-gen zee for
What's your favorite?	**Was ist ihr Lieblingsessen?**	vahs ist eer **leeb**-lings-es-sen
Is it...?	**Ist es...?**	ist es
...good	**...gut**	goot
...expensive	**...teuer**	**toy**-er
...light	**...leicht**	līkht
...filling	**...sättigend**	**set**-tee-gend
What's cheap and filling?	**Was ist billig und sättigend?**	vahs ist **bil**-lig oont **set**-tee-gend
What is fast?	**Was geht schnell?**	vahs gayt shnel
What is local?	**Was ist typisch?**	vahs ist **tew**-pish
What is that?	**Was ist das?**	vahs ist dahs
Do you have...?	**Haben Sie...?**	**hah**-ben zee
...an English menu	**...eine Speisekarte auf englisch**	ī-neh **shpī**-zeh-kar-teh owf **eng**-lish
...a children's portion	**...einen Kinderteller**	ī-nen **kin**-der-tel-ler

EATING

In many bars and restaurants you'll see tables with little signs that say *Stammtisch* ("this table reserved for our regulars"). Don't sit there unless you're invited by a local.

The menu:

menu	**Karte, Speisekarte**	**kar**-teh, **shpī**-zeh-**kar**-teh
menu of the day	**Tageskarte**	**tah**-ges-kar-teh
tourist menu	**Touristenmenü**	too-**ris**-ten-meh-**new**
specialty of the house	**Spezialität des Hauses**	**shpayt**-see-ahl-ee-**tayt** des **how**-zes
drink menu	**Getränkekarte**	geh-**trenk**-eh-**kar**-teh
breakfast	**Frühstück**	**frew**-shtewk
lunch	**Mittagessen**	**mit**-tahg-es-sen
dinner	**Abendessen**	**ah**-bent-es-sen
appetizers	**Vorspeise**	**for**-shpī-zeh
bread	**Brot**	broht
salad	**Salat**	zah-**laht**
soup	**Suppe**	**zup**-peh
first course	**erster Gang**	**ehr**-ster gahng
main course	**Hauptspeise**	**howpt**-shpī-zeh
meat	**Fleisch**	flīsh
poultry	**Geflügel**	geh-**flew**-gel
seafood	**Meeresfrüchte**	**meh**-res-frewkh-teh
side dishes	**Beilagen**	**bī**-lah-gen
vegetables	**Gemüse**	geh-**mew**-zeh
cheese	**Käse**	**kay**-zeh
dessert	**Nachspeise**	**nahkh**-shpī-zeh
beverages	**Getränke**	geh-**trenk**-eh
beer	**Bier**	beer

wine	**Wein**	vīn
cover charge	**Eintritt**	īn-trit
service included	**mit Bedienung**	mit beh-**dee**-noong
service not included	**ohne Bedienung**	**oh**-neh beh-**dee**-noong
hot / cold	**warm / kalt**	varm / kahlt
with / without	**mit / ohne**	mit / **oh**-neh
and / or	**und / oder**	oont / **oh**-der

Dietary restrictions:

I'm allergic to...	**Ich bin allergisch gegen...**	ikh bin ah-**lehr**-gish **gay**-gen
I cannot eat...	**Ich darf kein... essen.**	ikh darf kīn... **es**-sen
...dairy products.	**...Milchprodukte**	millkh proh **dook** teh
...meat.	**...Fleisch**	flīsh
...pork.	**...Schweinefleisch**	**shvī**-neh-flīsh
...salt / sugar.	**...Salz / Zucker**	zahlts / **tsoo**-ker
I'm a diabetic.	**Ich bin Diabetiker.**	ikh bin dee-ah-**bet**-i-ker
Low cholesterol?	**Niedriger Cholesterin?**	**nee**-dri-ger koh-**les**-ter-in
No caffeine.	**Koffeinfrei.**	koh-fay-**in**-frī
No alcohol.	**Kein alkohol.**	kīn **ahl**-koh-hohl
I'm a...	**Ich bin...**	ikh bin
...vegetarian.	**...Vegetarier.**	veh-geh-**tar**-ee-er
...strict vegetarian.	**...strenger Vegetarier.**	**shtreng**-er veh-geh-**tar**-ee-er
...carnivore.	**...Fleischfresser.**	**flīsh**-fres-ser

Tableware and condiments:

plate	**Teller**	**tel**-ler
napkin	**Serviette**	zehr-vee-**et**-teh
knife	**Messer**	**mes**-ser
fork	**Gabel**	**gah**-bel
spoon	**Löffel**	**lurf**-fel
cup	**Tasse**	**tah**-seh
glass	**Glas**	glahs
carafe	**Karaffe**	kah-**rah**-fah
water	**Wasser**	**vah**-ser
bread	**Brot**	broht
large pretzels	**Bretzeln**	**bret**-seln
butter	**Butter**	**but**-ter
margarine	**Margarine**	mar-gah-**ree**-neh
salt / pepper	**Salz / Pfeffer**	zahlts / **fef**-fer
sugar	**Zucker**	**tsoo**-ker
artificial sweetener	**Süßstoff**	**sews**-shtohf
honey	**Honig**	**hoh**-nig
mustard...	**Senf...**	zenf
...mild / sharp / sweet	**...mild / scharf /süß**	milled / sharf / zews
mayonnaise	**Mayonnaise**	mah-yoh-**nay**-zeh
ketchup	**Ketchup**	"ketchup"

German restaurants close one day a week. It's called
Ruhetag (quiet day). Before tracking down a recommended
restaurant, call to make sure it's open.

Restaurant requests and regrets:

A little.	Ein bißchen.	īn **bis**-yen
More. / Another.	Mehr. / Noch ein.	mehr / nokh īn
The same.	Das gleiche.	dahs **glīkh**-eh
I did not order this.	Dies habe ich nicht bestellt.	deez **hah**-beh ikh nikht beh-**shtelt**
Is it included with the meal?	Ist das im Essen eingeschlossen?	ist dahs im **es**-sen īn-geh-shlos-sen
I'm in a hurry.	Ich habe wenig Zeit.	ikh **hah**-beh **vay**-nig tsīt
I must leave at ___.	Ich muß um ___ gehen.	ikh mus oom ___ **gay**-hen
When will the food be ready?	Wann ist das Essen fertig?	vahn ist dahs **es**-sen **fehr**-tig
I've changed my mind.	Ich möchte das doch nicht.	ikh **murkh**-teh dahs dokh nikht
Can I get it "to go"?	Zum Mitnehmen?	tsoom **mit**-nay-men
This is...	Dies ist...	deez ist
...dirty.	...schmutzig.	**shmut**-tsig
...too greasy.	...zu fettig.	tsoo **fet**-tig
...too salty.	...zu salzig.	tsoo **zahl**-tsig
...undercooked.	...zu wenig gekocht.	tsoo **vay**-nig geh-**kokht**
...overcooked.	...zu lang gekocht.	tsoo lahng geh-**kokht**
...inedible.	...nicht eßbar.	nikht **es**-bar
...cold.	...kalt.	kahlt
Heat this up?	Dies aufwärmen?	deez **owf**-vehr-men
Enjoy your meal!	Guten Appetit!	**goo**-ten ah-peh-**teet**

EATING

Enough.	**Genug.**	geh-**noog**
Finished.	**Fertig.**	**fehr**-tig
Do any of your customers return?	**Kommen ihre Kunden je zurück?**	**kom**-men **eer**-eh **koon**-den yay tsoo-**rewk**
Yuck!	**Igitt!**	ee-**git**
Delicious!	**Lecker!**	**lek**-er
It tastes very good!	**Schmeckt sehr gut!**	shmekht zehr goot
Excellent!	**Ausgezeichnet!**	ows-get-**sīkh**-net

Paying for your meal:

Waiter / Waitress.	**Kellner / Kellnerin.**	**kel**-ner / **kel**-ner-in
Bill, please.	**Rechnung, bitte.**	**rekh**-noong **bit**-teh
Separate checks.	**Getrennte Rechnung.**	geh-**tren**-teh **rekh**-noong
Together.	**Zusammen.**	tsoo-**zah**-men
Credit card O.K.?	**Kreditkarte O.K.?**	kreh-**deet**-kar-teh "O.K."
Is there a cover charge?	**Kostet es Eintritt?**	**kos**-tet es **īn**-trit
This is not correct.	**Dies stimmt nicht.**	deez shtimt nikht
Please explain.	**Erklären Sie, bitte.**	ehr-**klehr**-en zee **bit**-teh
What if I wash the dishes?	**Und wenn ich die Teller abwasche?**	oont ven ikh dee **tel**-ler **ahp**-vah-sheh
Keep the change.	**Stimmt so.**	shtimt zoh
This is for you.	**Dies ist für Sie.**	deez ist fewr zee

When you're ready for the bill, ask for the *"Rechnung"* (reckoning). The service charge is always included. Tipping is not expected, although it's good style to round up the bill.

Breakfast:

breakfast	**Frühstück**	**frew**-shtewk
bread	**Brot**	broht
roll (Germany, Austria)	**Brötchen, Semmel**	**brurt**-khen, **zem**-mel
toast	**Toast**	tohst
butter	**Butter**	**but**-ter
jelly	**Gelee**	jeh-**lee**
pastry	**Kuchen**	**kookh**-en
croissant	**Butterhörnchen**	**but**-ter-hurn-khen
omelet	**Omelett**	**om**-let
eggs	**Eier**	**ī**-er
fried eggs	**Splegeleier**	**shpee**-gel-ī-er
scrambled eggs	**Rühreier**	**rew**-rī-er
soft boiled / hard boiled	**weichgekocht / hartgekocht**	**vɪkh**-geh-kokht / **hart**-geh-kokht
ham	**Schinken**	**shink**-en
bacon	**Speck**	shpek
cheese	**Käse**	**kay**-zeh
yogurt	**Joghurt**	**yoh**-gurt
cereal	**Cornflakes**	"cornflakes"
granola cereal	**Müsli**	**mews**-lee
milk	**Milch**	milkh
hot chocolate	**Heißer Schokolade**	**hī**-ser shoh-koh-**lah**-deh
fruit juice	**Fruchtsaft**	**frookht**-zahft

orange juice (fresh)	**Orangensaft (frischgepreßt)**	oh-**rahn**-jen-zahft (frish-geh-**prest**)
coffee / tea (see Drinking)	**Kaffee / Tee**	kah-**fay** / tee
Is breakfast included?	**Ist Frühstück eingeschlossen?**	ist **frew**-shtewk īn-geh-shlos-sen

Germans have an endearing and fun-to-mimic habit of greeting others in the breakfast room with a slow, miserable *"Morgen"* (Morning). If breakfast is optional, take a walk to the *Bäckerei-Konditorei* (bakery). Germany is famous for this special cultural attraction—more varieties of bread, pastries, and cakes than you ever imagined, baked fresh every morning and throughout the day. Sometimes a café is part of a *Konditorei*. For a hearty cereal, try *Bircher Müsli*, a healthy mix of oats and nuts.

Snacks and easy lunches:

toast with ham and cheese	**Toast mit Schinken und Käse**	tohst mit **shink**-en oont **kay**-zeh
bread with cheese	**Käsebrot**	**kay**-zeh-broht
sausage with...	**Wurst mit...**	vurst mit
...sauerkraut	**...Kraut**	krowt
...bread and mustard	**...Brot und Senf**	broht oont zenf
sandwich	**Sandwich**	**sahnd**-vich
vegetable platter	**Gemüseplatte**	geh-**mew**-zeh-plah-teh

Soups and salads:

soup	**Suppe**	**zup**-peh
soup of the day	**Suppe des Tages**	**zup**-peh des **tahg**-es
chicken broth...	**Hühnerbrühe...**	**hew**-ner-brew-heh
beef broth...	**Rinderbrühe...**	**rin**-der-brew-heh
...with noodles	**...mit Nudeln**	mit **noo**-deln
...with rice	**...mit Reis**	mit rīs
vegetable soup	**Gemüsesuppe**	geh-**mew**-zeh-zup-peh
goulash soup	**Gulaschsuppe**	**goo**-lahsh-zup-peh
liver dumpling soup	**Leberknödelsuppe**	**lay**-ber-kuh-nur-del-zup-peh
green salad	**grüner Salat**	**grew**-ner zah-**laht**
mixed salad	**gemischter Salat**	geh-**mish**-ter zah-**laht**
potato salad	**Kartoffelsalat**	kar-**tof**-fel-zah-laht
Greek salad	**Griechischer Salat**	**greekh**-ish-er zah-**laht**
chef's salad...	**gemischter Salat des Hauses...**	geh-**mish**-ter zah-**laht** des **how**-zes
...with ham and cheese	**...mit Schinken und Käse**	mit **shink**-en oont **kay**-zeh
...with egg	**...mit Ei**	mit ī
lettuce	**Salat**	zah-**laht**
tomatoes	**Tomaten**	toh-**mah**-ten
cucumber	**Gurken**	**gur**-ken
oil / vinegar	**Öl / Essig**	url / **es**-sig
salad dressing	**Salatsoße**	zah-**laht**-zoh-seh

dressing on the side	**Salatsoße extra**	zah-**laht**-zoh-seh **ehk**-strah
What is in	**Was ist in**	vahs ist in
this salad?	**diesem Salat?**	**dee**-zem zah-**laht**

The *Salatbar* (salad bar) is a global phenomenon. Budget travelers eat cheap and healthy by grabbing a plate and stacking it high. You'll normally be charged by the size of the plate for one load. Choose a *Teller* (plate) that is *kleiner* (small), *mittlerer* (medium), or *großer* (large). A small plate with a salad "pagoda" can make a fine and filling lunch.

Seafood:

seafood	**Meeresfrüchte**	meh-res-frewkh-teh
assorted seafood	**gemischte**	geh-**mish**-teh
	Meeresfrüchte	meh-res-frewkh-teh
fish	**Fisch**	fish
tuna	**Thunfisch**	tun-fish
herring	**Hering**	**hehr**-ing
clams	**Muscheln**	**moo**-sheln
cod	**Dorsch**	dorsh
trout	**Forelle**	foh-**rel**-leh
Where did this live?	**Wo hat dieses Tier gelebt?**	voh haht **dee**-zes teer geh-**laypt**
Just the head, please.	**Nur den Kopf, bitte.**	noor dayn kopf **bit**-teh

Poultry and meat:

poultry	**Geflügel**	geh-**flew**-gel
chicken	**Hähnchen**	**haynkh**-en
roast chicken	**Brathänchen**	**braht**-hayn-khen
turkey	**Pute**	**poo**-teh
duck	**Ente**	**en**-teh
meat	**Fleisch**	flīsh
mixed grill	**Grillteller**	**gril**-tel-ler
beef	**Rindfleisch**	rint-**flīsh**
roast beef	**Rinderbraten**	**rin**-der-brah-ten
beef steak	**Beefsteak**	**beef**-shtayk
veal	**Kalbfleisch**	**kahlp**-flīsh
cutlet	**Kotelett**	**kot**-let
pork	**Schweinefleisch**	**shvī**-neh-flīsh
ham	**Schinken**	**shink**-en
sausage	**Wurst**	vurst
bacon	**Speck**	shpek
lamb	**Lamm**	lahm
bunny	**Kaninchen**	kah-**neen**-khen
organs	**Innereien**	in-neh-**rī**-en
brains	**Brägen**	**breh**-gen
liver	**Leber**	**lay**-ber
tripe	**Kutteln**	**kut**-teln
How long has this been dead?	**Wie lange ist dieses Tier schon tot?**	vee **lahng**-eh ist **dee**-zes teer shohn toht

How it's prepared:

hot / cold	**heiß / kalt**	hīs / kahlt
raw / cooked	**roh / gekocht**	roh / geh-**kokht**
assorted	**gemischte**	geh-**mish**-teh
baked	**gebacken**	geh-**bah**-ken
boiled	**gekocht**	geh-**kokht**
deep-fried	**frittiert**	**frit**-ti-ert
fillet	**Filet**	fi-**lay**
fresh	**frisch**	frish
fried	**gebraten**	geh-**brah**-ten
grilled	**gegrillt**	geh-**grilt**
homemade	**hausgemachte**	hows-geh-**mahkh**-teh
in cream sauce	**in Rahmsauce**	in **rahm**-zohs
microwave	**Mikrowelle**	**mee**-kroh-vel-leh
mild	**mild**	milled
mixed	**gemischte**	geh-**mish**-teh
poached	**pochieren**	pohkh-**ee**-ren
roast	**Braten**	**brah**-ten
roasted	**geröstet**	geh-**rurs**-tet
sautéed	**sauté**	**sow**-tay
smoked	**geräuchert**	geh-**roykh**-ert
spicy hot	**scharf**	sharf
steamed	**gedünstet**	geh-**dewn**-stet
stuffed	**gefüllt**	geh-**fewlt**
sweet	**süß**	zews

Avoiding mis-steaks:

raw	**roh**	roh
rare	**halbgar**	**hahlp**-gar
medium	**mittel**	**mit**-tel
well-done	**durchgebraten**	**durkh**-geh-brah-ten
almost burnt	**fast verkohlt**	fahst fehr-**kohlt**

Styles of cooking:

art	style of cooking
Bauern	farmer style, with potatoes (good and hearty)
Jäger	hunter style, with mushrooms and gravy
Wiener	Viennese, breaded and fried
Französisch	French
Italienisch	Italian

Eating Italian in Germany:

Italian restaurants provide a good budget break from *wurst und kraut*. Here are the words you'll find on the menu: *Spaghetti, Pizza, Tomaten, Schinken* (ham), *Käse* (cheese), *Champignons* (mushrooms), *Paprika* (peppers), *Ei* (egg), *Pepperoni* (small hot peppers), *Zwiebeln* (onions), *Artischocken* (artichokes), *Basilikum* (basil), *Meeresfrüchte* (seafood), *Muscheln* (clams), and *Vegetaria* (vegetarian).

German specialties:

Brotzeit-Teller	plate of assorted meats and cheeses
Fleischfondue	meat cubes cooked in a pot of boiling oil and dipped in sauces
Fondue (Switz.)	bread cubes dipped in a mixture of melted cheese and white wine
Handkäse	curd cheese
Knödel	dense dumpling
Leberkäse	high quality Spam
Maultaschen	meat- or cheese-filled ravioli (grilled or in soup)
Raclette (Switz.)	melted cheese, ham, boiled potatoes, and pickle
Rösti (Switz.)	hashbrowns
Sauerbraten	braised beef, marinated in vinegar
Schlachtplatte	assorted cold meats (schlachten = slaughter, Schlacht = battle)
Schnitzel	thin slice of pork or veal, usually breaded
Schwarzwälder Schinken	smoked, cured ham

The best of the wurst:

Blutwurst	made from (gulp!) blood
Bratwurst	pork sausage, 2 inches in diameter, grilled or fried
Nürnberger	spicy pork sausage, grilled or fried, smaller than a hot dog
Schweinewurst	pork sausage

Weisswurst	white boiled veal that falls apart when you cut it. Don't eat the skin!	
mit Brot	with bread	
mit Kraut	with sauerkraut	

Side dishes:

vegetables	**Gemüse**	geh-**mew**-zeh
rice	**Reis**	rīs
spaghetti	**Spaghetti**	shpah-**geh**-tee
noodles	**Nudeln**	**noo**-deln
boiled German-style noodles	**Spätzle**	**shpets**-leh
liver / bread...	**Leber / Semmel...**	**lay**-ber / **zem**-mel
...dumplings	**...knödel**	kuh-**nur**-del
sauerkraut	**Sauerkraut**	"sauerkraut"
sliced pancakes	**Frittaten**	fri-**tah**-ten
potatoes	**Kartoffeln**	kar-**tof**-feln
French fries	**Pommes frites**	pom frits
potato salad	**Kartoffelsalat**	kar-**tof**-fel-zah-laht
green salad	**grüner Salat**	**grew**-ner zah-**laht**
mixed salad	**gemischter Salat**	geh-**mish**-ter zah-**laht**

Veggies and beans:

vegetables	**Gemüse**	geh-**mew**-zeh
mixed vegetables	**gemischtes Gemüse**	geh-**mish**-tes geh-**mew**-zeh
artichoke	**Artischocke**	art-i-**shoh**-keh
asparagus	**Spargel**	**shpar**-gel
beans	**Bohnen**	**boh**-nen
beets	**Rote Beete**	**roh**-teh **bee**-teh
broccoli	**Brokkoli**	**brok**-koh-lee
cabbage	**Kohl**	kohl
carrots	**Karotten**	kah-**rot**-ten
cauliflower	**Blumenkohl**	**bloo**-men-kohl
corn	**Mais**	mīs
cucumber	**Gurken**	**gur**-ken
eggplant	**Aubergine**	oh-behr-zhee-neh
French fries	**Pommes frites**	pom frits
garlic	**Knoblauch**	kuh-**noh**-blowkh
green beans	**grüne Bohnen**	**grew**-neh **boh**-nen
lentils	**Linsen**	**lin**-zen
mushrooms	**Champignons**	**shahm**-pin-yohn
olives	**Oliven**	oh-**leev**-en
onions	**Zwiebeln**	**tsvee**-beln
peas	**Erbsen**	**ehrb**-zen
pepper...	**Paprika...**	**pah**-pree-kah
...green / red / yellow	**...grün / rot / gelb**	grewn / roht / gelp
pickles	**Essiggurken**	**es**-sig-goor-ken
potatoes	**Kartoffeln**	kar-**tof**-feln

radishes	**Radieschen**	rah-**dee**-shen
spinach	**Spinat**	**shpee**-naht
tomatoes	**Tomaten**	toh-**mah**-ten
zucchini	**Zuccini**	**tsoo**-kee-nee

If you knead bread:

EATING

bread	**Brot**	broht
dark bread	**Vollkornbrot**	**fol**-korn-broht
three-grain bread	**Dreikornbrot**	**drī**-korn-broht
rye bread	**Roggenmischbrot**	**roh**-gen-mish-broht
dark rye bread	**Schwarzbrot**	**shvartz**-broht
whole wheat bread	**Graubrot**	**grow**-broht
light bread	**Weißbrot**	**vīs**-broht
wimpy white bread	**Toast**	tohst
French bread	**Baguette**	hah-**get**
roll (Germany, Austria)	**Brötchen, Semmel**	**brurt**-khen, **zem**-mel

Say cheese:

cheese	**Käse**	**kay**-zeh
mild / sharp	**mild / scharf**	milled / sharf
cheese platter	**Käseplatte**	**kay**-zeh-**plah**-teh
gorgonzola	**Gorgonzola**	**gor**-gon-tsoh-lah
bleu cheese	**Blaukäse**	**blow**-kay-zeh
cream cheese	**Frischkäse**	**frish**-kay-zeh
Swiss cheese	**Emmentaler**	**em**-men-tah-ler
a strong cheese	**Bergkäse**	**berg**-kay-zeh
Can I taste it?	**Kann ich probieren?**	kahn ikh **proh**-beer-en

Fruits and nuts:

almond	**Mandel**	**mahn**-del
apple	**Apfel**	**ahp**-fel
apricot	**Aprikose**	ahp-ri-**koh**-zeh
banana	**Banane**	bah-**nah**-neh
berries	**Beeren**	**behr**-en
canteloupe	**Melone**	meh-**loh**-neh
cherry	**Kirsche**	**keer**-sheh
chestnut	**Kastanie**	**kahs**-tah-nee
coconut	**Kokosnuß**	**koh**-kohs-noos
date	**Dattel**	**daht**-tel
fig	**Feige**	**fī**-geh
fruit	**Obst**	ohpst
grapefruit	**Pampelmuse**	**pahm**-pel-moo-zeh
grapes	**Trauben**	**trow**-ben
hazelnut	**Haselnuß**	**hah**-zel-noos
lemon	**Zitrone**	tsee-**troh**-neh
orange	**Apfelsine**	ahp-fel-**zee**-neh
peach	**Pfirsich**	**feer**-zikh
peanut	**Erdnuß**	**ehrd**-noos
pear	**Birne**	**beer**-neh
pineapple	**Ananas**	**ahn**-ahn-ahs
pistachio	**Pistazien**	pis-**tahts**-ee-en
plum	**Pflaume**	**flow**-meh
prune	**Backpflaume**	**bahk**-flow-meh

raspberry	**Himbeere**	**him**-behr-eh
red currants	**Johannisbeeren**	yoh-**hahn**-nis-behr-en
strawberry	**Erdbeere**	**ehrt**-behr-eh
tangerine	**Mandarine**	mahn-dah-**ree**-neh
walnut	**Wallnuß**	**vahl**-noos
watermelon	**Wassermelone**	**vah**-ser-meh-loh-neh

Teutonic treats:

dessert	**Nachspeise**	**nahkh**-shpī-zeh
strudel	**Strudel**	**shtroo**-del
cake	**Torte**	**tor**-teh
sherbet	**Sorbet**	zor-**bet**
fruit cup	**Früchtebecher**	**frewkh**-teh-bekh-er
tart	**Törtchen**	**turt**-khen
pie	**Kuchen**	**kookh**-en
cream	**Schlag**	shlahg
whipped cream	**Schlagsahne**	**shlahg**-zah-neh
chocolate mousse	**Mousse**	moos
pudding	**Pudding**	"pudding"
pastry	**Gebäck**	geh-**bek**
cookies	**Kekse**	**kayk**-zeh
candy	**Bonbons**	**bon**-bonz
low calorie	**kalorienarm**	kah-loh-**ree**-en-arm
homemade	**hausgemacht**	**hows**-geh-mahkht
Delicious!	**Köstlich! Lecker!**	**kurst**-likh / **lek**-er

EATING

| Heavenly. | **Himmlisch.** | **him**-lish |
| I'm in seventh heaven. | **Ich bin im siebten Himmel.** | ikh bin im **zeeb**-ten **him**-mel |

Ice cream:

ice cream	**Eis**	īs
scoop	**Kugel**	**koog**-el
cone	**Waffel**	**vah**-fel
small bowl	**Becher**	**bekh**-er
chocolate	**Schokolade**	shoh-koh-**lah**-deh
vanilla	**Vanille**	vah-**nil**-leh
strawberry	**Erdbeere**	**ehrt**-behr-eh
lemon	**Zitrone**	tsee-**troh**-neh
rum-raisin	**Malaga**	**mah**-lah-gah
hazelnut	**Haselnuß**	**hah**-zel-noos
Can I taste it?	**Kann ich probieren?**	kahn ikh **proh**-beer-en

Two great dessert specialties are Vienna's famous super chocolate cake, *Sachertorte,* and the Black Forest cherry cake called *Schwarzwälder Kirschtorte*. This diet-killing chocolate cake with cherries and rum can be found all over Germany. Chocoholics can pick up a jar of Nutella at any grocery store. Anything dipped in Nutella becomes a tasty souvenir. For a little bit of Italy, try *gelato* (Italian ice cream) at a *gelateria*.

Drinking

Water and juice:

mineral water...	**Mineralwasser...**	min-eh-**rahl**-vah-ser
...with / without carbonation	**...mit / ohne Kohlensäure**	mit / **oh**-neh koh-len-zoy-reh
mixed with mineral water	**gespritzt**	geh-**shpritzt**
tap water	**Leitungswasser**	lī-toongs-vah-ser
Fanta & Coke mix	**Mezzo Mix, Spezi**	**met**-soh mix, **shpet**-see
fruit juice	**Fruchtsaft**	**frookht**-zahft
apple juice	**Apfelsaft**	**ahp**-fel-zahft
orange juice (fresh)	**Orangensaft (frischgepreßt)**	oh-**rahn**-jen-zahft (frish-geh-**prest**)
with / without...	**mit / ohne...**	mit / **oh**-neh
...ice / sugar	**...Eis / Zucker**	īs / **tsoo**-ker
glass / cup	**Glas / Tasse**	glahs / **tah**-seh
small / large	**kleine / große**	**klī**-neh / **groh**-seh
bottle	**Flasche**	**flah**-sheh
Is the water safe to drink?	**Ist das Trinkwasser?**	ist dahs **trink**-vahs-ser

On a menu, you'll find drinks listed under *Getränkekarte* (drink menu). If you ask for *Wasser* in a restaurant, you'll be served mineral water. Free tap water is *Leitungswasser*. Germans normally don't drink this at the table. If you want *Leitungswasser*, be persistent.

EATING

Milk:

milk	**Milch**	milkh
whole milk	**Vollmilch**	**fol**-milkh
skim milk	**Magermilch**	**mah**-ger-milkh
fresh milk	**frische Milch**	**frish**-eh milkh
acidophilus	**acidophilus**	ah-see-**dof**-i-lus
buttermilk	**Buttermilch**	**but**-ter-milkh
chocolate milk	**Schokomilch**	**shoh**-koh-milkh
hot chocolate	**Heiße Schokolade**	**hī**-seh shoh-koh-**lah**-deh
milkshake	**Milchshake**	**milkh**-shayk

Coffee and tea:

coffee	**Kaffee**	kah-**fay**
espresso	**Espresso**	es-**pres**-soh
cappucino	**Cappucino**	kah-poo-**chee**-noh
iced coffee	**Eiskaffee**	**īs**-kah-fay
instant	**Pulverkaffee, Nescafe**	pool-ver-kah-**fay**, "nescafe"
decaffeinated	**koffeinfrei, Hag**	koh-fay-**in**-frī, hahg
black	**schwarz**	shvarts
with cream / milk	**mit Sahne / Milch**	mit **zah**-neh / milkh
with sugar	**mit Zucker**	mit **tsoo**-ker
hot water	**heißes Wasser**	**hī**-ses **vah**-ser
tea / lemon	**Tee / Zitrone**	tee / tsee-**troh**-neh
tea bag	**Teebeutel**	**tee**-boy-tel

iced tea	**Eistee**	īs-tee
herbal tea	**Kräutertee**	kroy-ter-tee
little pot	**Kännchen**	kaynkh-en
small / big	**klein / groß**	klīn / grohs
Another cup.	**Noch eine Tasse.**	nokh ī-neh tah-seh

In Austria, coffee has a language of its own. Ask for a *Brauner* to get coffee with cream, a *Melange* for coffee with lots of milk, a *Mokka* for black espresso, and *Obers* for cream.

Wine:

I would like...	**Ich hätte gern...**	ikh het-teh gehrn
We would like...	**Wir hätten gern...**	veer het-ten gehrn
...an eighth liter	**...ein Achtel**	īn ahkh-tel
...a quarter liter	**...ein Viertel**	īn feer-tel
...a carafe	**...eine Karaffe**	ī-neh kah-rah-feh
...a half bottle	**...eine halbe Flasche**	ī-neh hahl-beh flah-sheh
...a bottle	**...eine Flasche**	ī-neh flah-sheh
...of red wine	**...Rotwein**	roht-vīn
...of white wine	**...Weißwein**	vīs-vīn
...the wine list	**...die Weinkarte**	dee vīn-kar-teh

Typically you order a glass of wine by saying *"Ein Viertel"* (a quarter liter) or *"Ein Achtel"* (eighth liter).

Wine words:

wine	**Wein**	vīn
table wine	**Tafelwein**	**tah**-fel-vīn
house wine	**Hausmarke**	**hows**-mar-keh
local	**einheimisch**	**īn**-hī-mish
red wine	**Rotwein**	**roht**-vīn
white wine	**Weißwein**	**vīs**-vīn
rosé	**rosé**	roh-**zay**
sparkling	**sprudelnd**	**shproo**-delnd
sweet	**süß**	zews
medium	**halbtrocken**	**hahlp**-trok-en
(very) dry	**(sehr) trocken**	(zehr) **trok**-en
wine spritzer	**Wein gespritzt**	vīn geh-**shpritzt**
cork	**Korken**	**kor**-ken

Types of German wines:

Apfelwein	apple wine (Frankfurt)
Spätlese, Auslese, Beerenauslese, Trockenbeeren Auslese, Eiswein	sweet late harvest wines (listed from sweet to sweetest)
Kabinett	select wine
Qualitätswein	better quality wine
Qualitätswein mit Prädikat	best quality wine
Grüner Veltliner	popular Austrian wine
Heuriger	new wine
Schnaps	high-alcohol brandy (firewater!)
Kirschschnaps	high-alcohol cherry brandy

Nearly all German wines are white. You can identify the origin of the wine by the color or shape of the bottle: brown (Rhine), green (Mosel), jug-shaped (Franconian). As you travel through wine-growing regions, you'll see *probieren* signs inviting you in for a free (or nearly free) wine tasting.

Beer:

beer	**Bier**	beer
from the tap	**vom Faß**	fom fahs
bottle	**Flasche**	**flah**-sheh
light (Germany, Austria)	**helles, Märzen**	**hel**-les, **mehr**-tzen
dark	**dunkles**	**doonk**-les
local / imported	**einheimisch / importiert**	**in**-hi-mish / im-por-tee-**ert**
small / large	**kleines / großes**	**klī**-nes / **groh**-ses
half-liter	**Halbes**	**hahl**-bes
liter	**Mass**	mahs
alcohol-free	**alkoholfrei**	ahl-koh-hohl-**frī**
low calorie	**Light**	"light"
cold / colder	**kalt / kälter**	kahlt / **kel**-ter

Germany is Europe's beer capital. *Pils* is barley-based, *Weizen* is wheat-based, and *Malzbier* is the non-alcoholic malt beer that children learn on. *Radler* is a refreshing mix of beer and lemonade, and a *Berliner Weisse mit Schuß* is a wheat beer with a shot of fruit syrup. Drink menus list exactly how many deciliters you'll get in your glass. A "5 dl" beer is half a liter or about a pint. When you order beer, ask for *"Ein Halbes"* for a half liter or *"Ein Mass"* for a whole liter. Some beer halls serve beer only by the liter (about a quart)! Children are welcome in beer halls.

Bar talk:

What would you like?	**Was darf ich bringen?**	vahs darf ikh **bring**-en
What is the local specialty?	**Was ist die Spezialität hier?**	vahs ist dee **shpayt**-see-ahl-ee-**tayt** heer
Straight.	**Pur.**	poor
With / Without...	**Mit / Ohne...**	mit / **oh**-neh
...alcohol.	**...Alkohol.**	**ahl**-koh-hohl
...ice.	**...Eis.**	īs
One more.	**Noch eins.**	nokh īns
Cheers!	**Prost!**	prohst
To your health!	**Auf ihre Gesundheit!**	owf **eer**-eh geh-**zoond**-hīt
To you!	**Zum Wohl!**	tsoom vohl
Long life!	**Langes Leben!**	**lahng**-es **lay**-ben
I'm feeling...	**Ich bin...**	ikh bin
...a little drunk.	**...ein bißchen betrunken.**	īn **bis**-yen beh-**trunk**-en
...blitzed. (colloq.)	**...völlig blau.**	**fol**-lig blow

For drinks at reasonable prices, do what the locals do. Visit an atmospheric *Weinstube* (wine bar) or *Biergarten* (beer garden) and have a drink and chat with friends.

Picnicking

At the grocery:

Self-service?	**Selbstbedienung?**	**zelpst**-beh-dee-noong
Ripe for today?	**Jetzt reif?**	yetst rīf
Does this need to be cooked?	**Muß man das kochen?**	mus mahn dahs **kokh**-en
Can I taste it?	**Kann ich probieren?**	kahn ikh proh-**beer**-en
Fifty grams.	**Fünfzig Gramm.**	**fewnf**-tsig grahm
One hundred grams.	**Hundert Gramm.**	**hoon**-dert grahm
More. / Less.	**Mehr. / Weniger.**	mehr / **vay**-nig-er
A piece.	**Ein Stück.**	īn shtewk
A slice.	**Eine Scheibe.**	ī-neh shī-beh
Sliced.	**In Scheiben.**	in shī-ben
Can you make me a sandwich?	**Können Sie mir ein belegtes Brot machen?**	**kurn**-nen zee meer īn beh-**leg**-tes broht **mahkh**-en
To take out.	**Zum Mitnehmen.**	tsoom **mit**-nay-men
Is there a park nearby?	**Gibt es einen Park in der Nähe?**	gipt es ī-nen park in dehr **nay**-heh
Okay to picnic here?	**Darf man hier picknicken?**	darf mahn heer **pik**-nik-en
Enjoy your meal!	**Guten Appetit!**	**goo**-ten ah-peh-**teet**

You can assemble your picnic at a *Markt* (open air market) or *Supermarkt* (supermarket). Buy meat and cheese by the gram. One hundred grams is about a quarter pound, enough for two sandwiches. To get real juice, look for "100%" or "kein Zucker" on the label.

Tasty picnic words:

open air market	**Markt**	markt
grocery store	**Lebensmittelgeschäft**	lay-bens-mit-tel-geh-**sheft**
supermarket	**Supermarkt**	**zoo**-per-markt
picnic	**Picknick**	**pik**-nik
sandwich	**belegtes Brot**	beh-**leg**-tes broht
bread	**Brot**	broht
roll (Germany, Austria)	**Brötchen, Semmel**	**brurt**-khen, **zem**-mel
sausage	**Wurst**	vurst
ham	**Schinken**	**shink**-en
cheese	**Käse**	**kay**-zeh
mild / sharp / sweet	**mild / scharf / süß**	milled / sharf / zews
mustard...	**Senf...**	zenf
mayonnaise...	**Mayonnaise...**	mah-yoh-**nay**-zeh
...in a tube	**...in Tube**	in **too**-beh
yogurt	**Joghurt**	**yoh**-gurt
fruit	**Obst**	ohpst
box of juice	**Karton Saft**	**kar**-ton zaft
cold drinks	**kalte Getränke**	**kahl**-teh geh-**trenk**-eh
plastic...	**Plastik...**	**plahs**-tik
...spoon / fork	**...löffel / gabel**	**lurf**-fel / **gah**-bel
paper...	**Papier...**	pah-**peer**
...plate / cup	**...teller / becher**	**tel**-ler / **bekh**-er

German-English Menu Decoder

This handy decoder won't list every word on the menu, but it'll get you *Bratwurst* (pork sausage) instead of *Blutwurst* (blood sausage).

Abendessen dinner
Achtel eighth liter
Ananas pineapple
Apfel apple
Apfelsaft apple juice
Apfelsine orange
Aprikose apricot
Artischocke artichoke
Aubergine eggplant
Backpflaume prune
Banane banana
Bauern with potatoes
Becher small bowl
Bedienung service
Beeren berries
Beilagen side dishes
Bier beer
Birne pear
Blumenkohl cauliflower
Blutwurst blood sausage
Bohnen beans
braten roast
Brathähnchen roast chicken

Bratwurst pork sausage
Bretzeln pretzels
Brokkoli broccoli
Brot bread
Brötchen roll
Brotzeit snack
Butterhörnchen croissant
Champignons mushrooms
chinesisches Chinese
Dattel date
Dorsch cod
dunkles dark
Ei egg
Eier eggs
eingeschlossen included
einheimisch local
Eintritt cover charge
Eis ice cream
Eiskaffee iced coffee
Eistee iced tea
Ente duck
Erbsen peas
Erdbeere strawberry

Erdnuß peanut
erster Gang first course
Essen food
Essig vinegar
Essiggurken pickles
Feige fig
Fett fat
Fisch fish
Flasche bottle
Fleisch meat
Forelle trout
Französisch French
frisch fresh
frischgepreßt freshly squeezed
Frittaten sliced pancakes
frittiert deep-fried
Früchtebecher fruit cup
Fruchtsaft fruit juice
Frühstück breakfast
Gang course
Gebäck pastry
gebraten fried
gedünstet steamed
Geflügel poultry
gefüllt stuffed
gegrillt grilled
gekocht cooked
Gelee jelly
gemischte mixed

Gemüse vegetables
Gemüseplatte vegetable platter
geräuchert smoked
geröstet roasted
gespritzt with mineral water
Getränke beverages
Getränkekarte drink menu
Glas glass
Graubrot whole wheat bread
Grillteller mixed grill
groß big
grüner green
Gurken cucumber
Hähnchen chicken
halb half
hartgekocht hard-boiled
Haselnuß hazelnut
Hauptspeise main course
Haus house
hausgemachte homemade
heiß hot
helles light (beer)
Hering herring
Himbeere raspberry
Honig honey
Hühnerbrühe chicken broth
importiert imported
Innereien organs
Italienisch Italian

Jäger with mushrooms and gravy
Joghurt yogurt
Johannisbeeren red currant
Kaffee coffee
Kakao cocoa
Kalbfleisch veal
kalt cold
Kaninchen bunny
Kännchen small pot of tea
Karaffe carafe
Karotten carrots
Karte menu
Kartoffeln potatoes
Käse cheese
Käseplatte cheese platter
Kastanie chestnut
Kekse cookies
Kinderteller children's portion
Kirsche cherry
klein small
Kleinigkeit snack
Knoblauch garlic
Knödel dumpling
Kohl cabbage
Kohlensäure carbonation
Kokosnuß coconut
köstlich delicious
Kotelett cutlet
Kraut sauerkraut

Kräutertee herbal tea
Kugel scoop
Kutteln tripe
Lamm lamb
Leber liver
leicht light
Linsen lentils
Mais corn
Malaga rum-raisin flavor
Mandarine tangerine
Mandel almond
Mass liter of beer
Maultaschen ravioli
Meeresfrüchte seafood
Melone cantaloupe
Miesmuscheln mussels
Mikrowelle microwave
Milch milk
mild mild
Mineralwasser mineral water
mit with
Mittagessen lunch
Muscheln clams
Müsli granola cereal
Nachspeise dessert
Nudeln noodles
Obst fruit
oder or
ohne without

Öl oil
Oliven olives
Omelett omelet
Orangensaft orange juice
Pampelmuse grapefruit
Paprika bell pepper
Pfeffer pepper
Pfirsich peach
Pflaume plum
Pistazien pistachio
pochieren poached
Pommes frites French fries
Pute turkey
Raclette potatoes and cheese (Switz.)
Radieschen radishes
Rahmsauce cream sauce
Rinderbraten roast beef
Rinderbrühe beef broth
Rindfleisch beef
Roggenmischbrot rye bread
roh raw
Rösti hashbrowns (Switz.)
Rote Beete beets
Rotwein red wine
Rührreier scrambled eggs
Salat salad
Salatsoße salad dressing
Salz salt

sättigend filling
Sauerbraten braised beef
Schalentiere shellfish
scharf spicy
Scheibe slice
Schinken ham
Schlachtplatte assorted cold meats
Schlag cream
Schlagsahne whipped cream
schnell fast
Schnellimbiss fast food
Schnitzel thinly-sliced pork or veal
Schokolade chocolate
Schwarzbrot dark rye bread
Schweinefleisch pork
sehr very
Semmel roll
Senf mustard
Sorbet sherbet
Spargel asparagus
Spätzle German-style noodles
Speck bacon
Spezialität speciality
Spiegeleier fried eggs
Spinat spinach
sprudelnd sparkling
Stück piece
Suppe soup

süß   sweet
Tage   day
Tageskarte   menu of the day
Tasse   cup
Tee   tea
Teller   plate
Thunfisch   tuna
Tomaten   tomatoes
Törtchen   tart
Torte   cake
Trauben   grapes
trocken   dry
typisch   local
und   and
Vanille   vanilla
Vegetarier   vegetarian
Viertel   quarter liter
Vollkornbrot   dark bread
Vorspeise   appetizers

Waffel   cone
Wallnuß   walnut
Wasser   water
Wassermelone   watermelon
weichgekocht   soft-boiled
Wein   wine
Weinkarte   wine list
Weißwein   white wine
Wiener   breaded and fried
Wiesswurst   boiled veal sausage
Wurst   sausage
Zitrone   lemon
Zuccini   zucchini
Zucker   sugar
zum Mitnehman   "to go"
Zwiebelbraten   pot roast with
   onions
Zwiebeln   onions

MENU DECODER

Sightseeing

Where is...?	**Wo ist...?**	voh ist
...the best view	**...der beste Ausblick**	dehr **bes**-teh **ows**-blick
...the main square	**...der Hauptplatz**	dehr **howpt**-plahts
...the old town center	**...die Altstadt**	dee **ahlt**-shtaht
...the museum	**...das Museum**	dahs moo-**zay**-um
...the castle	**...die Burg**	dee burg
...the palace	**...das Schloß**	dahs shlos
...the ruins	**...die Ruine**	dee roo-**ee**-neh
...a fair (rides, games)	**...ein Jahrmarkt**	īn **yar**-markt
...a festival (music)	**...ein Festival**	īn fes-tee-**vahl**
...the tourist information office	**...das Touristen-informationsbüro**	dahs **too**-ris-ten-in-for-maht-see-**ohns**-bew-roh
Do you have...?	**Haben Sie...?**	**hah**-ben zee
...a city map	**...einen Stadtplan**	**ī**-nen **shtaht**-plahn
...brochures	**...Broschüren**	**broh**-shewr-en
...guidebooks	**...Führer**	**fewr**-er
...tours	**...Führungen**	**few**-roong-en
...in English	**...auf englisch**	owf **eng**-lish
When is the next tour in English?	**Wann ist die nächste Führung auf englisch?**	vahn ist dee **nekh**-steh **few**-roong owf **eng**-lish
Is it free?	**Ist es umsonst?**	ist es oom-**zonst**
How much is it?	**Wieviel kostet das?**	vee-**feel kos**-tet dahs

Is there a discount for...?	**Gibt es Ermäßigung für...?**	gipt es ehr-**may**-see-goong fewr
...youth	**...Kinder**	**kin**-der
...students	**...Studenten**	shtoo-**den**-ten
...seniors	**...Senioren**	zen-**yor**-en
Is the ticket good all day?	**Gilt die Karte den ganzen Tag lang?**	gilt dee **kar**-teh dayn **gahn**-tsen tahg lahng
Can I get back in?	**Kann ich wieder hinein?**	kahn ikh **vee**-der hin-**īn**
What time does this...?	**Um wieviel Uhr ist hier...?**	oom vee-**feel** oor ist heer
...open	**...geöffnet**	geh-**urf**-net
...close	**...geschlossen**	geh-**shlos**-sen
When is the last entry?	**Wann ist letzter Einlaß?**	vahn ist **lets**-ter **īn**-lahs
I beg of you, PLEASE let me in!	**BITTE, ich flehe Sie an, lassen Sie mich hinein!**	**bit**-teh ikh **flay**-heh zee ahn, **lah**-sen zee mikh hin-**īn**
I've traveled all the way from...	**Ich bin extra aus... gekommen.**	ikh bin **ehk**-strah ows... geh-**kom**-men
I must leave tomorrow.	**Ich muß morgen abreisen.**	ikh mus **mor**-gen **ahp**-rī-zen
I promise I'll be fast.	**Ich verspreche, mich zu beeilen.**	ikh fehr-**shprekh**-eh mikh tsoo **bay**-ī-len

SIGHTSEEING

In the museum:

Where is...?	**Wo ist...?**	voh ist
I'd like to see...	**Ich möchte gerne... sehen.**	ikh **murkh**-teh **gehr**-neh... **zay**-hen
Photos / videos O.K.?	**Fotografieren / filmen O.K.?**	foh-toh-grah-**feer**-en / **fil**-men "O.K."
No flash / tripod.	**Blitzlicht / Stativ verboten.**	**blits**-likht / shtah-**teef** fehr-**boh**-ten
I like it.	**Es gefällt mir.**	es geh-**felt** meer
It's so...	**Es ist so...**	es ist zoh
...beautiful.	**...schön.**	shurn
...ugly.	**...häßlich.**	**hes**-likh
...strange.	**...seltsam.**	**zelt**-zahm
...boring.	**...langweilig.**	**lahng**-vī-lig
...interesting.	**...interessant.**	in-tehr-es-**sahnt**
Wow!	**Fantastisch! Toll!**	fahn-**tahs**-tish / tol
My feet have had it!	**Meine Füße sind ganz plattgelaufen!**	**mī**-neh **few**-seh zint gahnts **plaht**-geh-**lowf**-en
I'm exhausted!	**Ich bin fertig!**	ikh bin **fehr**-tig

Be careful when planning your sightseeing. Many museums close one day a week and many stop selling tickets 45 minutes or so before they close. Many sights are only shown to groups with a guide. Individuals usually end up with the next German escort. To get an English tour, call in advance to see if one's scheduled. Individuals can often tag along with a large tour group.

Art and architecture:

art	**Kunst**	kunst
artist	**Künstler**	**kewnst**-ler
painting	**Gemälde**	geh-**mayl**-deh
self portrait	**Selbstporträt**	**zelpst**-por-tray
sculptor	**Bildhauer**	**bilt**-how-er
sculpture	**Skulptur**	**skulp**-toor
architect	**Architekt**	**arkh**-i-tekt
architecture	**Architektur**	**arkh**-i-tek-toor
original	**Original**	oh-rig-ee-**nahl**
restored	**restauriert**	res-tow-**ree**-ert
B.C.	**vor Christus**	for **kris**-tus
A.D.	**nach Christus**	nahkh **kris**-tus
century	**Jahrhundert**	yar-**hoon**-dert
style	**Stil**	shteel
Abstract	**Abstrakt**	ahp-**strahkt**
Ancient	**Altertümlich**	**ahl**-ter-tewm-likh
Art Nouveaux	**Jugendstil**	**yoo**-gend-shteel
Baroque	**Barock**	bah-**rok**
Classical	**Klassisch**	**klah**-sish
Gothic	**Gothisch**	**goh**-tish
Impressionist	**Impressionistisch**	im-preh-see-oh-**nis**-tish
Medieval	**Mittelalterlich**	**mit**-tel-ahl-ter-likh
Modern	**Modern**	moh-**dehrn**
Neoclassical	**Neoklassizistisch**	**nay**-oh-klah-sits-is-tish

Renaissance	**Renaissance**	**ren**-ah-sahns
Romanesque	**Romanisch**	roh-**mahn**-ish
Romantic	**Romantik**	roh-**mahn**-tik

Castles and palaces:

castle	**Burg**	burg
palace	**Schloß**	shlos
kitchen	**Küche**	**kewkh**-en
cellar	**Keller**	**kel**-ler
dungeon	**Verlies**	**fehr**-lees
moat	**Burggraben**	**burg**-grah-ben
fortified wall	**Burgmauer**	**burg**-mow-er
tower	**Turm**	turm
fountain	**Brunnen**	**brun**-nen
garden	**Garten**	**gar**-ten
king	**König**	**kur**-nig
queen	**Königin**	**kur**-nig-in
knights	**Ritter**	**rit**-ter

You'll see the words *burg* (castle) and *berg* (mountain) linked to the end of names (such as Rothenburg and Ehrenberg). Salzburg means "salt-castle."

Religious words:

cathedral	**Kathedrale**	kah-tee-**drah**-leh
church	**Kirche**	**keerkh**-eh
monastery	**Kloster**	**klohs**-ter
synagogue	**Synagoge**	zin-ah-**goh**-geh
chapel	**Kapelle**	kah-**pel**-leh
altar	**Altar**	ahl-**tar**
cross	**Kreuz**	kroyts
crypt	**Krypte**	**krip**-teh
treasury	**Schatzkammer**	**shots**-kah-mer
dome	**Kuppel**	**kup**-pel
bells	**Glocken**	**glok**-en
organ	**Orgel**	**org**-el
relic	**Reliquie**	reh-**leek**-wee-eh
saint	**Heiliger**	**hī**-lig-or
God	**Gott**	got
Jewish	**jüdisch**	**yew**-dish
Moslem	**Moslem**	**moz**-lem
Christian	**christlich**	**krist**-likh
Protestant	**evangelisch**	eh-vahn-**gay**-lish
Catholic	**katholisch**	kah-**toh**-lish
agnostic	**agnostisch**	ahg-**nohs**-tish
atheist	**atheistisch**	ah-tay-**is**-tish
When is the service?	**Wann ist der Gottesdienst?**	vahn ist dehr **got**-tes-deenst
Are there church concerts?	**Gibt es Kirchen-konzerte?**	gipt es keerkh-en-kon-**tsehr**-teh

Shopping

Names of shops:

antiques	**Antiquitäten**	ahn-tee-kwee-**tay**-ten
art gallery	**Kunstgalerie**	kunst-gah-leh-**ree**
bakery	**Bäckerei**	bek-eh-rī
barber shop	**Herrenfrisör**	hehr-ren-friz-**ur**
beauty salon	**Damenfrisör**	dah-men-friz-**ur**
book shop	**Buchladen**	**bookh**-lah-den
camera shop	**Photoladen**	**foh**-toh-lah-den
department store	**Kaufhaus**	**kowf**-hows
flea market	**Flohmarkt**	**floh**-markt
flower market	**Blumenmarkt**	**bloo**-men-markt
grocery store	**Lebensmittelgeschäft**	**lay**-bens-mit-tel-geh-**sheft**
hardware store	**Eisenwarengeschäft**	ī-zen-**vah**-ren-geh-**sheft**
jewelry shop	**Schmuckladen**	**shmuk**-lah-den
laundromat	**Waschsalon**	**vahsh**-zah-lon
newsstand	**Zeitungsstand**	**tsī**-toongs-shtahnt
office supplies	**Bürobedarf**	**bew**-roh-beh-darf
open air market	**Markt**	markt
optician	**Optiker**	**ohp**-ti-ker
pharmacy	**Apotheke**	ah-poh-**tay**-keh
photocopy shop	**Copyshop**	"copy shop"
shopping mall	**Shopping Center**	"shopping center"
souvenir shop	**Andenkenladen**	**ahn**-denk-en-**lah**-den

supermarket	**Supermarkt**	**zoo**-per-markt
toy store	**Spielzeugladen**	**shpeel**-tsoyg-lah-den
travel agency	**Reiseagentur**	rī-zeh-ah-gen-tur
used bookstore	**Bücher aus zweiter Hand**	**bookh**-er ows **tsvī**-ter hahnd
wine shop	**Weinhandlung**	**vīn**-hahnd-loong

Many businesses close from 12:00 to 15:00 on weekday afternoons and all day on Sundays. Typical hours are Monday through Friday 9:00 to 18:00, Saturday 9:00 to 13:00. Some stores stay open Thursdays until 21:00.

Shop till you drop:

sale	Ausverkauf	ows-fehr-kowf
special	Angebot	**ahn**-geh-boht
good value	preiswert	**prīs**-vehrt
How much is it?	Wieviel kostet das?	vee-**feel kos**-tet dahs
I'm just browsing.	Ich sehe mich nur um.	ikh **zay**-heh mikh noor oom
We're just browsing.	Wir sehen uns nur um.	veer **zay**-hen uns noor oom
I'd like...	Ich möchte...	ikh **murkh**-teh
Do you have...?	Haben Sie...?	hah-ben zee
...more	...mehr	mehr
...something cheaper	...etwas billigeres	et-vahs **bil**-lig-er-es
This one.	Dieses.	**dee**-zes

SHOPPING

Can I try it on?	**Kann ich es anprobieren?**	kahn ikh es **ahn**-proh-beer-en
Do you have a mirror?	**Haben Sie einen Spiegel?**	**hah**-ben zee ī-nen **shpee**-gel
Too...	**Zu...**	tsoo
...big.	**...groß.**	grohs
...small.	**...klein.**	klīn
...expensive.	**...teuer.**	**toy**-er
Did you make this?	**Haben Sie das gemacht?**	**hah**-ben zee dahs geh-**mahkht**
What is it made out of?	**Was ist das für Material?**	vahs ist dahs fewr mah-ter-ee-**ahl**
Machine washable?	**Waschmaschinen-fest?**	**vahsh**-mah-sheen-en-fest
Will it shrink?	**Läuft es ein?**	loyft es īn
Credit card O.K.?	**Kreditkarte O.K.?**	kreh-**deet**-kar-teh "O.K."
Can you ship this?	**Können Sie das versenden?**	**kurn**-nen zee dahs fehr-**zen**-den
Tax-free?	**Steuerfrei?**	**shtoy**-er-frī
I'll think about it.	**Ich denk drüber nach.**	ikh denk **drew**-ber nahkh
What time do you close?	**Um wieviel Uhr schließen Sie?**	oom vee-**feel** oor **shlee**-sen zee
What time do you open tomorrow?	**Wann öffnen Sie morgen?**	vahn **urf**-nen zee **mor**-gen
Is that your lowest price?	**Ist das der günstigste Preis?**	ist dahs dehr **gewn**-stig-steh prīs

My last offer.	**Mein letztes Angebot.**	mīn **lets**-tes **ahn**-geh-boht
I'm nearly broke.	**Ich bin fast pleite.**	ikh bin fahst **plī**-teh
My male friend...	**Mein Freund...**	mīn froynd
My female friend...	**Meine Freundin...**	**mī**-neh **froyn**-din
My husband...	**Mein Mann...**	mīn mahn
My wife...	**Meine Frau...**	**mī**-neh frow
...has the money.	**...hat das Geld.**	haht dahs gelt

For colors and fabrics, see the dictionary near the end of this book.

SHOPPING

Repair:

These handy lines can apply to any repair, whether it's a cranky zipper, broken leg, or dying car.

This is broken.	**Das hier ist kaputt.**	dahs heer ist kah-**put**
Can you fix it?	**Können Sie das reparieren?**	**kurn**-nen zee dahs reh-pah-**reer**-en
Just do the essentials.	**Machen Sie nur das Wichtigste.**	**mahkh**-en zee noor dahs **vikh**-tig-steh
How much will it cost?	**Wieviel kostet das?**	vee-**feel kos**-tet dahs
When will it be ready?	**Wann ist es fertig?**	vahn ist es **fehr**-tig
I need it by ___.	**Ich brauche es um ___.**	ikh **browkh**-eh es oom ___

Entertainment

What's happening tonight?	**Was ist heute abend los?**	vahs ist **hoy**-teh **ah**-bent lohs
Can you recommend something?	**Können Sie etwas empfehlen?**	**kurn**-nen zee et-vahs emp-**fay**-len
Is it free?	**Ist es umsonst?**	ist es oom-**zohnst**
Where can I buy a ticket?	**Wo kann ich eine Karte kaufen?**	voh kahn ikh **ī**-neh **kar**-teh **kowf**-en
When does it start?	**Wann fängt es an?**	vahn fengt es ahn
When does it end?	**Wann endet es?**	vahn **en**-det es
Will you go out with me?	**Möchten Sie mit mir ausgehen?**	**murkh**-ten zee mit meer **ows**-gay-hen
Where's the best place to dance nearby?	**Wo geht man hier am besten tanzen?**	voh gayt mahn heer ahm **bes**-ten **tahn**-tsen
Do you want to dance?	**Möchten Sie tanzen?**	**murkh**-ten zee **tahn**-tsen
Again?	**Noch einmal?**	nokh **īn**-mahl
Let's party!	**Feiern wir!**	**fī**-ern veer

What's happening:

movie...	**Film...**	film
...original version	**...im Original**	im oh-rig-ee-**nahl**
...in English	**...auf englisch**	owf **eng**-lish
...with subtitles	**...mit Untertiteln**	mit **oon**-ter-tee-teln
...dubbed	**...übersetzt**	ew-behr-**zetst**

music...	Musik...	moo-**zeek**
...live	...**live**	"live"
...classical	...**klassisch**	**klahs**-sish
folk music	**Volksmusik**	**fohlks**-moo-zeek
old rock	**Alter Rock**	**ahl**-ter rok
jazz	**Jazz**	"jazz"
blues	**Blues**	"blues"
singer	**Sänger**	**zeng**-er
concert	**Konzert**	kon-**tsert**
show	**Vorführung**	for-**few-roong**
dancing	**Tanzen**	**tahn**-tsen
folk dancing	**Folkstanz**	**fohlks**-tahnts
disco	**Disko**	**dis**-koh
cover charge	**Eintritt**	**in**-trit

Oktoberfest, the famous Munich beer festival, fills Bavaria's capital with the sounds of *"Prost!"*, carnival rides, sizzling bratwurst, and oompah bands. The party starts the third Saturday in September and lasts for 16 days. The *Salzburger Festspiele* (Salzburg's music festival) gives visitors the sound of music from late July to the end of August. Each country's national tourist office in the U.S.A. can mail you a free schedule (in English) of upcoming festivals.

ENTERTAINMENT

Phoning

Where is the nearest phone?	**Wo ist das nächste Telefon?**	voh ist dahs **nekh**-steh tel-eh-**fohn**
I'd like to telephone...	**Ich möchte einen Anruf nach... machen.**	ikh **murkh**-teh **ī**-nen **ahn**-roof nahkh... **mahkh**-en
...the U.S.A.	**...U.S.A.**	oo es ah
What is the cost per minute?	**Wieviel kostet es pro Minute?**	vee-**feel** kos-tet es proh mee-**noo**-teh
I'd like to make a... call.	**Ich möchte ein... machen.**	ikh **murkh**-teh īn... **mahkh**-en
...local	**...Ortsgespräch**	**orts**-geh-shpraykh
...collect	**...Rückgespräch**	**rewk**-geh-shpraykh
...credit card	**...Kreditkarten- gespräch**	kreh-**deet**-kar-ten- geh-shpraykh
...long distance	**...Ferngespräch**	**fehrn**-geh-shpraykh
It doesn't work.	**Es außer Betrieb.**	es **ow**-ser beh-**treep**
May I use your phone?	**Darf ich mal Ihr Telefon benutzen?**	darf ikh mahl eer tel-eh-**fohn** beh-**noo**-tsen
Can you dial for me?	**Können Sie für mich wählen?**	**kurn**-nen zee fewr mikh **vay**-len
Can you talk for me?	**Können Sie für mich sprechen?**	**kurn**-nen zee fewr mikh **shprekh**-en
It's busy.	**Besetzt.**	beh-**zetst**
Will you try again?	**Noch einmal versuchen?**	nokh **īn**-mahl fehr-**zookh**-en
Hello? (on phone)	**Ja, bitte?**	yah **bit**-teh

My name is...	**Ich heiße...**	ikh **hī**-seh
My number is...	**Meine Telefon-**	**mī**-neh tel-eh-**fohn-**
	nummer ist...	num-mer ist
Speak slowly.	**Sprechen Sie**	**shprekh**-en zee
	langsam.	**lahng**-zahm
Wait a moment.	**Moment.**	moh-**ment**
Don't hang up.	**Nicht auflegen.**	nikht **owf**-lay-gen

Key telephone words:

telephone	**Telefon**	tel-eh-**fohn**
telephone card	**Telefonkarte**	tel-eh-**fohn**-kar-teh
operator	**Vermittlung**	fehr-**mit**-loong
international	**Internationale**	in-tehr-naht-see-oh-**nah**-leh
assistance	**Auskunft**	**ows**-koonft
country code	**Landesvorwahl**	**lahn**-des-for-vahl
area code	**Vorwahl**	**for**-vahl
telephone book	**Telefonbuch**	tel-eh-**fohn**-bookh
yellow pages	**Gelbe Seiten**	**gehlp**-eh **zī**-ten
toll-free	**gebührenfrei**	geh-**bew**-ren-frī
out of service	**Außer Betrieb**	**ow**-ser beh-**treep**

In Germany, it's considered polite to identify yourself by
name at the beginning of every phone conversation. A
telephone card (*Telefonkarte*), available at post offices, is
handier than using coins for your calls. Post offices also
have easy-to-use metered phones. For more tips, see
"Let's Talk Telephones" near the end of this book.

PHONING

Mailing

Where is the post office?	**Wo ist das Postamt?**	voh ist dahs **post**-ahmt
Which window for...?	**An welchem Schalter ist...?**	ahn **vehlkh**-em **shahl**-ter ist
...stamps	**...Briefmarken**	**breef**-mar-ken
...packages	**...Pakete**	pah-**kay**-teh
To America....	**Nach Amerika...**	nahkh ah-**mehr**-ee-kah
...by air mail.	**...mit Luftpost.**	mit **luft**-post
...slow and cheap.	**...langsam und billig.**	**lahng**-zahm oont **bil**-lig
How much is it?	**Wieviel kostet das?**	vee-**feel kos**-tet dahs
How many days will it take?	**Wieviele Tage braucht das?**	vee-**fee**-leh **tahg**-eh browkht dahs

Licking the postal code:

German Postal Service	**Deutsche Bundespost**	**doy**-cheh **boon**-des-post
post office	**Postamt**	**post**-ahmt
stamp	**Briefmarke**	**breef**-mar-keh
postcard	**Postkarte**	**post**-kar-teh
letter	**Brief**	breef
aerogram	**Luftpostpapier**	**luft**-post-pah-**peer**
envelope	**Umschlag**	**oom**-shlahg
package	**Paket**	pah-**kayt**
box	**Karton**	kar-**ton**

string	**Schnur**	shnoor
tape	**Klebeband**	**klay**-beh-bahnd
mailbox	**Briefkasten**	**breef**-kahs-ten
air mail	**Luftpost**	**luft**-post
express mail	**Eilpost**	**īl**-post
slow and cheap	**langsam und billig**	**lahng**-zahm oont **bil**-lig
book rate	**Büchersendung**	**bewkh**-er-**zayn**-doong
weight limit	**Gewichtsbegren-zung**	geh-**vikhts**-beh-gren-tsoong
registered	**Einschreiben**	**īn**-shrī-ben
insured	**versichert**	fehr-**zikh**-ert
fragile	**zerbrechlich**	tsehr-**brekh**-likh
contents	**Inhalt**	**in**-hahlt
customs	**Zoll**	tsol
to	**nach**	nahkh
from	**von**	fon
address	**Adresse**	ah-**dres**-seh
zip code	**Postleitzahl**	**post**-līt-sahl
general delivery	**postlagernd**	**post**-lah-gehrnt

MAILING

In Germany, Austria, and Switzerland, you can often get stamps at the corner *Tabakladen* (tobacco shop). As long as you know which stamps you need, this is a great convenience.

To save money, mail your postcards outside of Germany. If you mail a package from Germany, consider *Economy Plus*. It's slower and cheaper than air mail, and faster than surface mail.

Red Tape & Profanity

Filling out forms:

Herr / Frau / Fräulein	Mr. / Mrs. / Miss
Vorname	first name
Name	name
Adresse	address
Wohnort	address
Straße	street
Stadt	city
Staat	state
Land	country
Nationalität	nationality
Herkunft / Reiseziel	origin / destination
Alter	age
Geburtsdatum	date of birth
Geburtsort	place of birth
Geschlecht	sex
männlich / weiblich	male / female
verheiratet / ledig	married / single
Beruf	profession
Erwachsener	adult
Kind / Junge / Mädchen	child / boy / girl
Kinder	children
Familie	family
Unterschrift	signature

German profanity:
In any country, red tape can lead to a blue streak. These words will help you understand what the more colorful locals are saying...

Damn it.	**Verdammt.**	fehr-**dahmt**
Shit.	**Scheiße.**	**shī**-seh
Go to hell.	**Geh zur Hölle.**	gay tsur **hurl**-leh
Screw it.	**Scheiß drauf.**	**shīs** drowf
Sit on it.	**Am Arsch.**	ahm arsh
bastard (pig-dog)	**Schweinehund**	**shvī**-neh-hoont
bitch (goat)	**Ziege**	**tsee**-geh
breasts (colloq.)	**Titten**	**tit**-en
penis (colloq.)	**Schwanz**	shvahnts
butthole	**Arschloch**	**arsh**-lokh
drunk	**besoffen**	beh-**zof**-fen
stupid (dumb head)	**Dummkopf**	**dum**-kopf
Did someone...?	**Hat jemand...?**	haht **yay**-mahnd
...burp	**...gerülpst**	geh-**rewlpst**
...fart	**...gefurzt**	geh-**furtst**

RED TAPE

Help!

Help!	**Hilfe!**	**hil**-feh
Help me!	**Helfen Sie mir!**	**hel**-fen zee meer
Call a doctor!	**Rufen Sie einen Arzt!**	**roo**-fen zee **ī**-nen artst
ambulance	**Krankenwagen**	**krahn**-ken-vah-gen
accident	**Unfall**	**oon**-fahl
injured	**verletzt**	fehr-**letst**
emergency	**Notfall**	**noht**-fahl
police	**Polizei**	poh-leet-**sī**
thief	**Dieb**	deep
pick-pocket	**Taschendieb**	**tahsh**-en-deep
I've been ripped off.	**Ich bin bestohlen worden.**	ikh bin beh-**shtoh**-len **vor**-den
I've lost my...	**Ich habe meine... verloren.**	ikh **hah**-beh **mī**-neh... fehr-**lor**-en
...passport.	**...Paß**	pahs
...ticket.	**...Karte**	**kar**-teh
...baggage.	**...Gepäck**	geh-**pek**
...purse.	**...Handtasche**	**hahnd**-tash-eh
...wallet.	**...Brieftasche**	**breef**-tash-eh
...faith in humankind.	**...Glauben an die Menschheit**	**glow**-ben ahn dee **mehnsh**-hīt
I'm lost.	**Ich habe mich verlaufen.**	ikh **hah**-beh mikh fehr-**lowf**-en

Help for women:

Leave me alone.	**Lassen Sie mich in Ruhe.**	**lah**-sen zee mikh in **roo**-heh
I *vant* to be alone.	**Ich möchte alleine sein.**	ikh **murkh**-teh ah-**lī**-neh zīn
I'm not interested.	**Ich hab kein Interesse.**	ikh hahp kīn in-tehr-**es**-seh
I'm married.	**Ich bin verheiratet.**	ikh bin fehr-**hī**-rah-tet
I'm a lesbian.	**Ich bin Lesbierin.**	ikh bin les-**beer**-in
I have a contagious disease.	**Ich habe eine ansteckende Krankheit.**	ikh **hah**-beh ī-neh **ahn**-shtek-en-deh **krahnk**-hīt
Don't touch me.	**Fassen Sie mich nicht an.**	**fah**-sen zee mikh nikht ahn
You're disgusting.	**Sie sind eklig.**	zee zint **ek**-lig
Stop following me.	**Hör auf, mir nachzulaufen.**	hur owf meer **nahkh**-tsoo-**lowf**-en
This man is bothering me.	**Der Mann stört mich.**	dehr mahn shturt mikh
Enough!	**Das reicht!**	dahs rīkht
Get lost!	**Hau ab!**	how ahp
Drop dead!	**Verschwinde!**	fehr-**shvin**-deh
I'll call the police.	**Ich rufe die Polizei.**	ikh **roo**-feh dee poh-leet-**sī**

HELP!

Health

I feel sick.	**Mir ist schlecht.**	meer ist shlekht
I need a doctor...	**Ich brauche einen Arzt...**	ikh **browkh**-eh ī-nen artst
...who speaks English.	**...der Englisch spricht.**	dehr **eng**-lish shprikht
It hurts here.	**Hier tut es weh.**	heer toot es vay
I'm allergic to...	**Ich bin allergisch gegen...**	ikh bin ah-**lehr**-gish **gay**-gen
...penicillin.	**...Penizillin.**	pen-ee-tsee-**leen**
I am diabetic.	**Ich bin Diabetiker.**	ikh bin dee-ah-**bet**-ee-ker
I've missed a period.	**Ich habe meine Tage nicht bekommen.**	ikh **hah**-beh mī-neh **tahg**-eh nikht beh-**kom**-men
My male friend has...	**Mein Freund hat...**	mīn froynd haht
My female friend has...	**Meine Freundin hat...**	mī-neh **froyn**-din haht
I have...	**Ich habe...**	ikh **hah**-beh
...a burn.	**...eine Verbrennung.**	ī-neh fehr-**bren**-noong
...chest pains.	**...Schmerzen in der Brust.**	**shmehrt**-sen in dehr brust
...a cold.	**...eine Erkältung.**	ī-neh ehr-**kel**-toong
...constipation.	**...Verstopfung.**	fehr-**shtop**-foong
...a cough.	**...einen Husten.**	ī-nen **hoo**-sten
...diarrhea.	**...Durchfall.**	**durkh**-fahl
...dizziness.	**...Schwindel.**	**shvin**-del
...a fever.	**...Fieber.**	**fee**-ber
...the flu.	**...die Grippe.**	dee **grip**-peh

...giggles.	...einen Lachanfall.	ī-nen **lahkh**-ahn-fahl
...hay fever.	...**Heuschnupfen.**	**hoysh**-nup-fen
...a headache.	...**Kopfschmerzen.**	**kopf**-shmehrt-sen
...hemorrhoids.	...**Hämorrholden.**	**hay**-mor-hohl-den
...high blood pressure.	...**Bluthochdruck.**	**bloot**-hokh-druk
...indigestion.	...**Verdauungsstörung.**	fehr-**dow**-oongs-shtur-oong
...an infection.	...**eine Entzündung.**	ī-neh **ent**-sewn-doong
...a migraine.	...**Migräne.**	mee-**gray**-neh
...nausea.	...**Übelkeit.**	**ew**-bel-kīt
...a rash.	...**einen Ausschlag.**	ī-nen **ows**-shlahg
...a sore throat.	...**Halsschmerzen.**	**hahls**-shmehrt-sen
...a stomach ache.	...**Magenschmerzen.**	**mah**-gen-shmehrt-sen
...a swelling.	...**eine Schwellung.**	ī-neh **shvel**-loong
...a toothache.	...**Zahnschmerzen.**	**tsahn**-shmehrt-sen
...a venereal disease.	...**eine Geschlechts-krankeit.**	ī-neh geh-**shlekhts**-krahn-kīt
...worms.	...**Würmer.**	**vewr**-mer
I have body odor.	**Ich habe Körpergeruch.**	ikh **hah**-beh **kur**-per-geh-rookh
Is it serious?	**Ist es ernst?**	ist es ehrnst

Handy health words:

pain	**Schmerz**	shmehrts
dentist	**Zahnarzt**	**tsahn**-artst
doctor	**Arzt**	artst
nurse	**Krankenschwester**	**krahn**-ken-shves-ter
health insurance	**Krankenversicherung**	**krahn**-ken-fehr-**zikh**-ch-roong

hospital	**Krankenhaus**	**krahn**-ken-hows
bandage	**Verband**	fehr-**bahnt**
medicine	**Medikamente**	med-ee-kah-**men**-teh
pharmacy	**Apotheke**	ah-poh-**tay**-keh
prescription	**Rezept**	reh-**tsehpt**
pill	**Pille**	**pil**-leh
aspirin	**Aspirin**	ah-spir-**een**
non-aspirin substitute	**Ben-u-ron**	**behn**-oo-ron
antibiotic	**Antibiotika**	ahn-tee-bee-**oh**-tee-kah
cold medicine	**Grippemittel**	**grip**-eh-mit-tel
cough drops	**Hustenbonbons**	**hoo**-sten-bohn-bohz
pain killer	**Schmerzmittel**	**shmehrts**-mit-tel
Preparation H	**Preparation H**	preh-pah-raht-see-**ohn** hah
vitamins	**Vitamine**	**vee**-tah-mee-neh

Glasses and contact lenses:

glasses	**Brille**	**bril**-leh
sunglasses	**Sonnenbrille**	**zoh**-nen-bril-leh
prescription	**Rezept**	reh-**tsept**
soft lenses	**Weiche Linsen**	**vīkh**-eh lin-zen
hard lenses	**Harte Linsen**	**har**-teh lin-zen
cleaning solution	**Reinigungslösung**	**rī**-nee-goongs-lur-zoong
soaking solution	**Kontaktlinsenbad**	kon-**tahkt**-lin-zen-baht
I've... a contact lens.	**Ich habe meine**	ikh **hah**-beh **mī**-neh
	Kontaktlinse...	kon-**tahkt**-lin-zeh
...lost	**...verloren.**	fehr-**lor**-en
...swallowed	**...verschluckt.**	fehr-**shlukt**

Toiletries:

comb	**Kamm**	kahm
conditioner	**Spülung**	**shpew**-loong
condoms	**Kondome**	**kohn**-doh-meh
dental floss	**Zahnseide**	**tsahn**-zī-deh
deodorant	**Deodorant**	deh-oh-doh-**rahnt**
hairbrush	**Haarbürste**	**har**-bewr-steh
hand lotion	**Handcreme**	**hahnd**-kreh-meh
lip salve	**Lippenpflege**	**lip**-pen-fleg-eh
nail clipper	**Nagelschere**	**nahg**-el-sheh-reh
razor	**Rasierer**	rah-**zeer**-er
sanitary napkins	**Damenbinden**	**dah**-men-bin-den
shampoo	**Shampoo**	**shahm**-poo
shaving cream	**Rasierseife**	rah-**zeer**-zī-feh
soap	**Seife**	**zī**-feh
sunscreen	**Sonnencreme**	**zoh**-nen-kreh-meh
tampons	**Tampons**	**tahm**-pohnz
tissues	**Taschentücher**	**tah**-shen-tewkh-er
toilet paper	**Klopapier**	kloh-pah-**peer**
toothbrush	**Zahnbürste**	**tsahn**-bewr-steh
toothpaste	**Zahnpasta**	**tsahn**-pah-stah
tweezers	**Pinzette**	pin-**tseh**-teh

HEALTH

Chatting

My name is...	**Ich heiße...**	ikh **hī**-seh
What's your name?	**Wie heißen Sie?**	vee **hī**-sen zee
How are you?	**Wie geht's?**	vee gayts
Very well, thanks.	**Sehr gut, danke.**	zehr goot **dahng**-keh
Where are you from?	**Woher kommen Sie?**	**voh**-hehr **kom**-men zee
What...?	**Von welcher...?**	fon **velkh**-er
...city	**...Stadt**	shtaht
...country	**...Land**	lahnd
...planet	**...Planet**	plahn-**et**
I'm from...	**Ich bin aus...**	ikh bin ows
...America.	**...Amerika.**	ah-**mehr**-i-kah
...Canada.	**...Kanada.**	**kah**-nah-dah

Nothing more than feelings...

I am / You are...	**Ich bin / Sie sind...**	ikh bin / zee zint
...happy.	**...glücklich.**	glewk-likh
...sad.	**...traurig.**	**trow**-rig
...tired.	**...müde.**	**mew**-deh
...hungry.	**...hungrig.**	**hoon**-grig
...thirsty.	**...durstig.**	**dur**-stig
I'm cold.	**Mir ist kalt.**	meer ist kahlt
I'm too warm.	**Mir ist zu warm.**	meer ist tsoo varm
I'm homesick.	**Ich habe Heimweh.**	ikh **hah**-beh **hīm**-vay
I'm lucky.	**Ich habe Glück.**	ikh **hah**-beh glewk

Who's who:

This is a... of mine.	**Das ist...von mir.**	dahs ist īn... fon meer
...male friend	**...ein Freund**	īn froynd
...female friend	**...eine Freundin**	ī-neh **froyn**-din
My...	**Mein / Meine...**	mīn / **mī**-neh
...boyfriend / girlfriend.	**...Freund / Freundin.**	froynd / **froyn**-din
...husband / wife.	**...Mann / Frau.**	mahn / frow
...son / daughter.	**...Sohn / Tochter.**	zohn / **tokh**-ter
...brother / sister.	**...Bruder / Schwester.**	**broo**-der / **shves**-ter
...father / mother.	**...Vater / Mutter.**	**fah**-ter / **mut**-ter
...uncle / aunt.	**...Onkel / Tante.**	**ohn**-kel / **tahn**-teh
...nephew / niece.	**...Neffe / Nichte.**	**nef**-feh / **neckh**-teh
...male / female cousin.	**...Cousin / Cousine.**	koo-**zeen** / koo-**zee**-neh
...grandfather / grandmother.	**...Großvater / Großmutter.**	**grohs**-fah-ter / **grohs**-mut-ter
...grandson / granddaughter.	**...Enkel / Enkelin.**	**en**-kel / **en**-kel-in

Family, school, and work:

Are you married?	**Sind Sie verheiratet?**	zint zee fehr-**hī**-rah-tet
Do you have children?	**Haben Sie Kinder?**	**hah**-ben zee **kin**-der
How many boys / girls?	**Wieviele Jungen / Mädchen?**	vee-**fee**-leh **yoong**-gen / **mayd**-khen
Do you have photos?	**Haben Sie Fotos?**	**hah**-ben zee **foh**-tohs
How old is your child?	**Wie alt ist Ihr Kind?**	vee ahlt ist eer kint

Beautiful child!	Schönes Kind!	shur-nes kint
Beautiful children!	Schöne Kinder!	shur-neh kin-der
What are you studying?	Was studieren Sie?	vahs shtoo-deer-en zee
I'm studying...	Ich studiere...	ikh shtoo-deer-eh
I'm... years old.	Ich bin... Jahre alt.	ikh bin... yah-reh ahlt
How old are you?	Wie alt sind Sie?	vee ahlt zint zee
Do you have siblings?	Haben Sie Geschwister?	hah-ben zee geh-shvis-ter
Will you teach me a simple German song?	Können Sie mir ein einfaches deutsches Lied beibringen?	kurn-nen zee meer īn īn-fahkh-es doy-ches leet bī-bring-gen
I'm a...	Ich bin...	ikh bin
...student. (male / female)	...Student / Studentin.	shtoo-dent / shtoo-dent-in
...teacher. (male / female)	...Lehrer / Lehrerin.	lehr-er / lehr-er-in
...worker.	...Arbeiter.	ar-bī-ter
...bureaucrat.	...Bürokrat.	bew-roh-kraht
...professional traveler.	...professioneller Reisender.	proh-fes-see-ohn-nel-ler rī-zen-der
What is your occupation?	Was machen Sie beruflich?	vahs mahkh-en zee beh-roof-likh
Do you like your work?	Gefällt Ihnen ihre Arbeit?	geh-felt ee-nen eer-eh ar-bīt

Travel talk:

I am / Are you...?	**Ich bin / Sind Sie...?**	ikh bin / zint zee
...on vacation	**...auf Urlaub**	owf **oor**-lowp
Are you working today?	**Arbeiten Sie heute?**	**ar**-bit-en zee **hoy**-teh
How long have you been traveling?	**Wie lange sind Sie schon im Urlaub?**	vee **lahng**-eh zint zee shohn im **oor**-lowp
day / week / month / year	**Tag / Woche / Monat / Jahr**	tahg / **vokh**-eh / **moh**-naht / yar
When are you going home?	**Wann fahren Sie zurück?**	vahn **far**-en zee tsoo-**rewk**
This is my first time in...	**Ich bin zum ersten Mal in...**	ikh bin tsoom **ehr**-sten mahl in
It's (not) a tourist trap.	**Es ist (nicht) nur für Touristen.**	es ist (nikht) noor fewr too-**ris**-ten
Today / Tomorrow I'm going to...	**Heute / Morgen fahre ich nach...**	**hoy**-teh / **mor**-gen **far**-eh ikh nahkh
I'm very happy here.	**Ich bin sehr glücklich hier.**	ikh bin zehr **glewk**-likh heer
The Germans / Austrians / Swiss...	**Die Deutschen / Österreicher / Schweizer...**	dee **doy**-chen / **urs**-teh-rīkh-er / **shvīt**-ser
...are very friendly.	**...sind sehr freundlich.**	zint zehr **froynd**-likh
This is a wonderful country.	**Dies ist ein wunderbares Land.**	deez ist īn **voon**-dehr-bah-res lahnd
Travel is good living.	**Auf Reisen lebt's sich gut.**	owf **rī**-zen laypts zikh goot
Have a good trip!	**Gute Reise!**	**goo**-teh **rī**-zeh

CHATTING

Map talk:

These phrases and maps will help you delve into family history and explore travel dreams.

I live here.	Ich wohne hier.	ikh **voh**-neh heer
I was born here.	Ich bin hier geboren.	ikh bin heer geh-**boh**-ren
My ancestors came from...	Meine Vorfahren kamen aus...	**mī**-neh **for**-far-en **kah**-men ows
I've traveled to...	Ich bin hier gewesen...	ikh bin heer geh-**vay**-zen
Next I'll go to...	Als nächstes gehe ich nach...	als **nekh**-stes **gay**-heh ikh nahkh
Where do you live?	Wo wohnen Sie?	voh **voh**-nen zee
Where were you born?	Wo sind Sie geboren?	voh zint zee geh-**boh**-ren
Where did your ancestors come from?	Woher kommen ihre Vorfahren?	**voh**-hehr **kom**-men **ee**-reh **for**-far-en
Where have you traveled?	Wo sind Sie schon gewesen?	voh zint zee shohn geh-**vay**-zen
Where are you going?	Wohin gehen Sie?	**voh**-hin **gay**-hen zee
Where would you like to go?	Wohin möchten Sie?	**voh**-hin **murkh**-ten zee

Germany

Austria

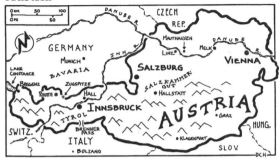

Switzerland

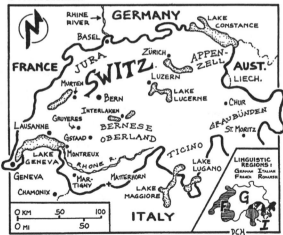

Weather:

What's the weather tomorrow?	**Wie wird das Wetter morgen?**	vee virt dahs **veht**-ter **mor**-gen
sunny / cloudy	**sonnig / bewölkt**	**zon**-nig / beh-**vurlkt**
hot / cold	**heiß / kalt**	hīs / kahlt
muggy / windy	**schwül / windig**	shvewl / **vin**-dig
rain / snow	**Regen / Schnee**	**ray**-gen / shnay

Favorite things:

What is your favorite...?	**Was ist Ihr Lieblings...?**	vahs ist eer **lee**-bleengs
...art	**...Kunst**	kunst
...artist	**...Künstler**	**kewnst**-ler
...author	**...Autor**	**ow**-tor
...book	**...Buch**	bookh
...music	**...Musik**	moo-**zeek**
...singer	**...Sänger**	**zeng**-er
...movie	**...Film**	"film"
...movie star	**...Filmstar**	"filmstar"
...food	**...Essen**	**es**-sen
...ice cream	**...Eis**	īs
...hobby	**...Hobby**	"hobby"
...sport	**...Sport**	shport
...vice	**...Sünde**	**zewn**-deh

Responses for all occasions:

I like that.	**Das gefällt mir.**	dahs geh-**felt** meer
I like you.	**Sie gefallen mir.**	zee geh-**fah**-len meer
That's cool!	**Na, super!**	nah **zoo**-per
Excellent!	**Ausgezeichnet!**	ows-get-**sīkh**-net
Perfect.	**Perfekt.**	per-**fekt**
Funny.	**Komisch.**	**koh**-mish
Interesting.	**Interessant.**	in-tehr-es-**sahnt**
I don't smoke.	**Ich rauche nicht.**	ikh **rowkh**-eh nikht
Really?	**Wirklich?**	**virk**-likh
Congratulations!	**Herzlichen Glückwunsch!**	**hehrts**-likh-en **glewk**-vunsh
Well done!	**Gut gemacht!**	goot geh-**mahkht**
You're welcome.	**Bitte schön.**	**bit**-teh shurn
Bless you! (after sneeze)	**Gesundheit!**	geh-**zoond**-hīt
Excuse me.	**Entschuldigung.**	ent-**shool**-dee-goong
What a pity.	**Wie schade.**	vee **shah**-deh
That's life.	**So geht's eben.**	zoh gayts **ay**-ben
No problem.	**Kein Problem.**	kīn proh-**blaym**
O.K.	**O.K.**	"O.K."
This is the good life!	**So ist das Leben schön!**	zoh ist dahs **lay**-ben shurn
Good luck!	**Viel Glück!**	feel glewk
Let's go!	**Auf geht's!**	owf gayts

CHATTING

Thanks a million:

Thank you very much.	**Vielen Dank.**	**fee**-len dahngk
You are...	**Sie sind...**	zee zint
...helpful.	**...hilfreich.**	**hilf**-rīkh
...wonderful.	**...wunderbar.**	**voon**-der-bar
...generous.	**...großzügig.**	**grohs**-tsew-gig
...hairy.	**...haarig.**	**hah**-rig
This is great fun.	**Das macht viel Spaß.**	dahs mahkht feel shpahs
You've gone to much trouble.	**Sie haben sich sovil Mühe gemacht.**	zee **hah**-ben sikh **zoh**-feel **mew**-heh geh-**mahkht**
You are an angel from God.	**Sie sind ein Engel, von Gott gesandt.**	zee zint īn **eng**-el fon got geh-**zahndt**
I will remember you...	**Ich werde Sie... in Erinnerung behalten.**	ikh **vehr**-deh zee... in ehr-**rin**-eh-roong beh-**hahl**-ten
...always.	**...immer**	**im**-mer
...till Tuesday.	**...bis Dienstag**	bis **deen**-stahg

Conversing with German animals:

rooster / cock-a-doodle-doo	**Hahn / kikeriki**	hahn / kee-keh-ree-**kee**
bird / tweet tweet	**Vogel / piep piep**	**foh**-gel / peep peep
cat / meow	**Katze / miau**	**kaht**-seh / mee-**ow**
dog / woof woof	**Hund / wuff wuff**	hoont / vuff vuff
duck / quack quack	**Ente / quak quak**	**en**-teh / kwahk kwahk
cow / moo	**Kuh / muh**	koo / moo
pig / oink oink	**Schwein / nöff nöff**	shvīn / nurf nurf

Create Your Own Conversation

You can mix and match these words into a conversation.
Make it as deep or silly as you want.

Who:

I / you	**ich / Sie**	ikh / zee
he / she	**er / sie**	er / zee
we / they	**wir / sie**	veer / zee
my / your...	**mein / ihre...**	mīn / eer
...parents / children	**...Eltern / Kinder**	**el**-tern / **kin**-der
men / women	**Männer / Frauen**	**men**-ner / **frow**-en
rich / poor	**Reichen / Armen**	**rīkh**-en / **ar**-men
politicians	**Politiker**	poh-**lit**-i-ker
big business	**Großkapital**	**grohs**-kahp-i-tahl
mafia	**Mafia**	**mah**-fee-ah
military	**Militär**	mil-ee-**tehr**
Neo-Nazis	**Neonazis**	"Neo-Nazis"
eastern Germany	**Ostdeutschland**	**ost**-doych-lahnd
western Germany	**Westen von Deutschland**	**ves**-ten fon **doych**-lahnd
Germans	**Deutschen**	**doy**-chen
Austrians	**Österreicher**	**urs**-teh-rīkh-er
Swiss	**Schweizer**	**shvīt**-ser
French	**Franzosen**	frahn-**tsoh**-zen
Italians	**Italiener**	i-tah-lee-**ehn**-er
Americans	**Amerikaner**	ah-mehr-ee-**kahn**-er

CHATTING

liberals	**Liberale**	**lib**-eh-rah-leh
conservatives	**Konservative**	**kohn**-zehr-vah-tiv-eh
radicals	**Radikale**	**rah**-di-kah-leh
travelers	**Reisende**	**rī**-zen-deh
everyone	**alle Leute**	**ah**-leh **loy**-teh
God	**Gott**	got

What:

want / need	**wollen / brauchen**	**vol**-len / **browkh**-en
take / give	**nehmen / geben**	**nay**-men / **gay**-ben
love / hate	**lieben / hassen**	**lee**-ben / **hah**-sen
work / play	**arbeiten / spielen**	**ar**-bīt-en / **shpeel**-en
have / lack	**haben / haben nicht**	**hah**-ben / **hah**-ben nikht
learn / fear	**lernen / fürchten**	**lern**-en / **fewrkh**-ten
help / abuse	**helfen / mißbrauchen**	**hel**-fen / mis-**broykh**-en
prosper / suffer	**florieren / leiden**	floh-**ree**-ren / **lī**-den
buy / sell	**kaufen / verkaufen**	**kow**-fen / **fehr**-kow-fen

Why:

love	**Liebe**	**lee**-beh
sex	**Sex**	sex
money	**Geld**	gelt
power	**Macht**	mahkht
work	**Arbeit**	**ar**-bīt

food	**Essen**	**es**-sen
family	**Familie**	fah-**mee**-lee-eh
health	**Gesundheit**	geh-**zoond**-hīt
hope	**Hoffnung**	**hof**-noong
education	**Ausbildung**	**ows**-bil-doong
guns	**Waffen**	**vah**-fen
religion	**Religion**	reh-leeg-ee-**ohn**
happiness	**Glück**	glewk
marijuana	**Marihuana**	**mah**-ri-wah-nah
democracy	**Demokratie**	day-moh-krah-**tee**
taxes	**Steuern**	**shtoy**-ern
lies	**Lügen**	**lew**-gen
corruption	**Korruption**	kor-rupt-see-**ohn**
pollution	**Umweltver-** **schmutzung**	**oom**-velt-fehr- **shmut**-tsoong
television	**Fernsehen**	fern-**zay**-hen
relaxation	**Entspannung**	ent-**shpah**-noong
violence	**Gewalt**	geh-**vahlt**
reunification	**Wiedervereinigung**	**vee**-dehr-fehr-īn-i-goong
respect	**Respekt**	res-**pekt**
racism	**Rassimus**	rah-**sis**-moos
war / peace	**Krieg / Frieden**	kreeg / **free**-den
global perspective	**Gesamtperspektive**	geh-**zahmt**-per-spek-ti-veh

CHATTING

You be the judge:

(no) problem	**(kein) Problem**	(kīn) proh-**blaym**
(not) good	**(nicht) gut**	(nikht) goot
(not) dangerous	**(nicht) gefährlich**	(nikht) geh-**fayr**-likh
(not) fair	**(nicht) fair**	(nikht) "fair"
(not) guilty	**(nicht) schuldig**	(nikht) **shool**-dig
(not) powerful	**(nicht) mächtig**	(nikht) **mekh**-tig
(not) stupid	**(nicht) dumm**	(nikht) dum
(not) happy	**(nicht) glücklich**	(nikht) **glewk**-likh
because / for	**weil / wegen**	vīl / **vay**-gen
and / or / from	**und / oder / von**	oont / **oh**-der / fon
too much	**zu viel**	tsoo feel
enough	**genug**	geh-**noog**
never enough	**nie genug**	nee geh-**noog**
worse	**schlechter**	**shlekh**-ter
same	**gleich**	glīkh
better	**besser**	**bes**-ser
here	**hier**	heer
everywhere	**überall**	ew-ber-**ahl**

Assorted beginnings and endings:

I like...	**Ich mag...**	ikh mahg
I don't like...	**Ich mag... nicht.**	ikh mahg... nikht
Do you like...?	**Mögen Sie...?**	**mur**-gen zee
In the past...	**Früher...**	**frew**-her
I am / Are you...?	**Ich bin / Sind Sie...?**	ikh bin / zint zee
...an optimist / pessimist	**...ein Optimist / Pessimist**	īn **opt**-i-meest / **pes**-i-meest
I believe in...	**Ich glaube an...**	ikh **glow**-beh ahn
I don't believe in...	**Ich glaube nicht an...**	ikh **glow**-beh nikht ahn
Do you believe in...?	**Glauben Sie an...?**	**glow**-ben zee ahn
...God	**...Gott**	got
...life after death	**...Leben nach dem Tod**	**lay** bon nahkh daym tod
...extraterrestrial life	**...Leben im Weltall**	**lay**-ben im **velt**-ahl
...Santa Claus	**...Weihnachtsmann**	**vī**-nahkhts-mahn
Yes. / No.	**Ja. / Nein.**	yah / nīn
Maybe.	**Vielleicht.**	fee-**līkht**
I don't know.	**Ich weiß nicht.**	ikh vīs nikht
What is most important in life?	**Was ist das Wichtigste im Leben?**	vahs ist dahs **vikh**-tig-steh im **lay**-ben
The problem is...	**Das Problem ist...**	dahs proh-**blaym** ist
The answer is...	**Die Antwort ist...**	dee **ahnt**-vort ist
We have solved the world's problems.	**Wir haben die Probleme der Welt gelöst.**	veer **hah**-ben dee proh-**blay**-meh dehr velt geh-**lurst**

A German Romance

Words of love:

I / me / you	**ich / mich / dich**	ikh / mikh / dikh
flirt	**flirten**	**flir**-ten
kiss	**Kuß**	kus
hug	**Umarmung**	oom-**ar**-mung
love	**Liebe**	**lee**-beh
make love (sleep together)	**zusammen schlafen**	tsoo-**zah**-men **shlah**-fen
condom	**Präservativ**	pray-zehr-fah-**tif**
contraceptive	**Verhütungsmittel**	fehr-**hew**-toongs-**mit**-tel
safe sex	**safe sex**	"safe sex"
sexy	**sexy**	"sexy"
cozy	**gemütlich**	geh-**mewt**-likh
romantic	**romantisch**	roh-**mahn**-tish
cupcake	**Schnuckel**	**shnuk**-el
little rabbit	**Häschen**	**hays**-khen
little sugar mouse	**Zuckermäuschen**	tsoo-ker-**moys**-khen
pussy cat	**Miezekatze**	meets-eh-**kaht**-seh

Ah, Liebe:

What's the matter?	**Was ist los?**	vahs ist lohs
Nothing.	**Nichts.**	nikhts

I am / Are you...?	Ich bin / Sind Sie...?	ikh bin / zint zee
...straight	...hetero	hay-ter-oh
...gay	...schwul	shvul
...undecided	...mir nicht sicher	meer nikht zikh-er
...prudish	...verklemmt	fehr-klemt
...horny	...geil	gīl
We are on our honeymoon.	Wir sind auf unserer Hochzeitsreise.	veer zint owf oon-zer-er hokh-tsīts-rī-zeh
I have...	Ich habe...	ikh hah-beh
...a boyfriend.	...einen Freund.	ī-nen froynd
...a girlfriend.	...eine Freundin.	ī-neh froyn-din
I am (not) married.	Ich bin (nicht) verheiratet.	ikh bin (nikht) fehr-hī-rah-tet
I am rich and single.	Ich bin reich und zu haben.	ikh bin rīkh oont tsoo hah-ben
I am lonely.	Ich bin einsam.	ikh bin īn-zahm
I have no diseases.	Ich habe keine Krankheiten.	ikh hah-beh kī-neh krahnk-hī-ten
I have many diseases.	Ich habe viele Krankheiten.	ikh hah-beh fee-leh krahnk-hī-ten
Can I see you again?	Können wir uns wiedersehen?	kurn-nen veer oons vee-der-zayn
You are my most beautiful souvenir.	Du bist mein schönstes Andenken.	doo bist mīn shurn-stes ahn-denk-en
Is this an aphrodisiac?	Ist dies ein Aphrodisiakum?	ist deez īn ah-froh-dee-zee-ahk-oom

CHATTING

This is (not) my first time.	**Dies ist für mich (nicht) das erste Mal.**	deez ist fewr mikh (nikht) dahs **ehr**-steh mahl
Do you do this often?	**Machst du das oft?**	mahkhst doo dahs oft
How's my breath?	**Habe ich Mundgeruch?**	**hah**-beh ikh **mund**-geh-rukh
Let's just be friends.	**Wir können doch einfach Freunde sein.**	veer **kurn**-nen dokh **īn**-fahkh **froyn**-deh zīn
I'll pay for my share.	**Ich bezahle meinen Anteil.**	ikh beht-**sah**-leh **mī**-nen **ahn**-tīl
Would you like a... massage?	**Darf ich dir den... massieren?**	darf ikh deer dayn... mah-**see**-ren
...foot	**...Fuß**	foos
...back	**...Rücken**	**rew**-ken
Why not?	**Warum nicht?**	vah-**room** nikht
Try it.	**Versuch's doch mal.**	fehr-**zookhs** dokh mahl
That tickles.	**Das kitzelt.**	dahs **kit**-selt
Oh my God!	**Oh mein Gott!**	oh mīn got
I love you.	**Ich liebe dich.**	ikh **lee**-beh dikh
Darling, marry me!	**Liebling, heirate mich!**	**lee**-bleeng **hī**-rah-teh mikh

English - German Dictionary

A

above über
accident Unfall
accountant Buchhalter
adaptor Zwischenstecker
address Adresse
adult Erwachsener
afraid ängstlich
after nach
afternoon Nachmittag
aftershave Rasierwasser
afterwards nachher
again noch einmal
age Alter
aggressive aggressiv
agree einverstanden
AIDS AIDS
air Luft
air-conditioned Klimaanlage
airline Fluggesellschaft
air mail Luftpost
airport Flughafen
alarm clock Wecker
alcohol Alkohol
allergic allergisch
allergies Allergien
alone allein
already schon
always immer

ancestor Vorfahre
ancient altertümlich
and und
angry wütend
ankle Fußknöchel
animal Tier
another noch ein
answer Antwort
antibiotic Antibiotika
antiques Antiquitäten
apartment Wohnung
apology Entschuldigung
appetizers Vorspeise
apple Apfel
appointment Verabredung
approximately ungefähr
arm Arm
arrivals Ankunften
arrive ankommen
art Kunst
artificial künstlich
artist Künstler
ashtray Aschenbecher
ask fragen
aspirin Aspirin
at bei
attractive attraktiv
aunt Tante
Austria Österreich
autumn Herbst

DICTIONARY

B

baby Baby
babysitter Babysitter
backpack Rucksack
bad schlecht
bag Tüte
baggage Gepäck
bakery Bäckerei
balcony Balkon
ball Ball
banana Banane
band-aid Pflaster
bank Bank
barber Frisör
basement Keller
basket Korb
bath Bad
bathroom Bad
bathtub Badewanne
battery Batterie
beach Strand
beard Bart
beautiful schön
because weil
bed Bett
bedroom Zimmer
bedsheet Laken
beef Rindfleisch
beer Bier
before vor
begin anfangen
behind hinter
below unter

belt Gürtel
best am besten
better besser
bib Lätzchen
bicycle Fahrrad
big groß
bill (payment) Rechnung
bird Vogel
birthday Geburtstag
black schwarz
blanket Decke
blond blond
blood Blut
blouse Bluse
blue blau
boat Schiff
body Körper
boiled gekocht
bomb Bombe
book Buch
book shop Buchladen
boots Stiefel
border Grenze
borrow leihen
boss Boss
bottle Flasche
bottom Boden
bowl Schale
box Karton
boy Junge
bra B.H.
bracelet Armband
bread Brot
breakfast Frühstück

bridge   Brücke
briefs   Unterhosen
Britain   England
broken   kaputt
brother   Bruder
brown   braun
bucket   Eimer
building   Gebäude
bulb   Birne
burn (n)   Verbrennung
bus   Bus
business   Geschäft
but   aber
button   Knopf
buy   kaufen
by (via)   mit

C

calendar   Kalender
calorie   Kalorie
camera   Photoapparat
camping   Camping
can (n)   Dose
can (v)   können
Canada   Kanada
can opener   Dosenöffner
canal   Kanal
candle   Kerze
candy   Bonbons
canoe   Kanu
cap   Deckel
captain   Kapitän
car   Auto

carafe   Karaffe
card   Karte
cards (deck)   Karten
careful   vorsichtig
carpet   Teppich
carry   tragen
cashier   Kassierer
cassette   Kassette
castle   Burg
cat   Katze
catch (v)   fangen
cathedral   Kathedrale
cave   Höhle
cellar   Keller
center   Zentrum
century   Jahrhundert
chair   Stuhl
change (n)   Wechsel
change (v)   wechseln
charming   bezaubernd
cheap   billig
check   Scheck
Cheers!   Prost!
cheese   Käse
chicken   Hühnchen
children   Kinder
Chinese (adj)   chinesisches
chocolate   Schokolade
Christmas   Weihnachten
church   Kirche
cigarette   Zigarette
cinema   Kino
city   Stadt
class   Klasse

clean (adj) sauber
clear klar
cliff Kliff
cloth Stoff
clothes Kleider
closed geschlossen
clothesline Wäscheleine
clothes pins Wäscheklammern
cloudy bewölkt
coast Küste
coat Jacke
coat hanger Kleiderbügel
coffee Kaffee
coins Münzen
cold (adj) kalt
colors Farben
comb (n) Kamm
come kommen
comfortable komfortabel
compact disc C.D.
complain sich beschweren
complicated kompliziert
computer Komputer
concert Konzert
condom Präservativ
conductor Schaffner
confirm konfirmieren
congratulations Glückwünsche
connection (train) Anschluß
constipation Verstopfung
cook (v) kochen
cool kühl
cork Korken
corkscrew Korkenzieher

corner Ecke
corridor Flur
cost (v) kosten
cot Liege
cotton Baumwolle
cough (v) husten
cough drops Hustenpastillen
country Land
countryside auf dem Land
cousin Vetter
cow Kuh
cozy gemütlich
crafts Kunstgewerbe
cream Sahne
credit card Kreditkarte
crib Kinderbett
crowd (n) Menge
cry (v) weinen
cup Tasse

D

dad Papa
dance (v) tanzen
danger Gefahr
dangerous gefährlich
dark dunkel
daughter Tochter
day Tag
dead tot
delay Verspätung
delicious lecker
dental floss Zahnseide
dentist Zahnarzt

deodorant   Deodorant
depart   abfahren
departures   Abfahrten
deposit   Kaution
dessert   Nachtisch
detour   Umleitung
diabetic   diabetisch
diamond   Diamant
diaper   Windel
diarrhea   Durchfall
dictionary   Wörterbuch
die   sterben
difficult   schwierig
dinner   Abendessen
direct   direkt
direction   Richtung
dirty   schmutzig
discount   Ermäßigung
disease   Krankheit
disturb   stören
divorced   geschieden
doctor   Arzt
dog   Hund
doll   Puppe
donkey   Esel
door   Tür
dormitory   Schlafsaal
double   doppel
down   runter
dream (n)   Traum
dream (v)   träumen
dress (n)   Kleid
drink (n)   Getränk
drive (v)   fahren

driver   Fahrer
drunk   betrunken
dry   trocken

E

each   jede
ear   Ohr
early   früh
earplugs   Ohrenschützer
earrings   Ohrringe
earth   Erde
east   Osten
Easter   Ostern
easy   einfach
eat   essen
elbow   Ellbogen
elevator   Fahrstuhl
embarrassing   peinlich
embassy   Botschaft
empty   leer
engineer   Ingenieur
English   Englisch
enjoy   genießen
enough   genug
entrance   Eingang
entry   Eingang
envelope   Briefumschlag
eraser   Radiergummi
especially   besonders
Europe   Europa
evening   Abend
every   jede
everything   alles

exactly genau
example Beispiel
excellent ausgezeichnet
except außer
exchange (n) Wechsel
excuse me Entschuldigung
exhausted erschöpft
exit Ausgang
expensive teuer
explain erklären
eye Auge

F

face Gesicht
factory Fabrik
fall (v) fallen
false falsch
family Familie
famous berühmt
fantastic phantastisch
far weit
farm Bauernhof
farmer Bauer
fashion Mode
fat (adj) fett
father Vater
father-in-law Schwiegervater
faucet Wasserhahn
female weiblich
ferry Fähre
festival Festival
fever Fieber
few wenig

field Feld
fight (n) Streit
fight (v) streiten
fine (good) gut
finger Finger
finish (v) beenden
fireworks Feuerwerk
first erst
first aid Erste Hilfe
first class erste Klasse
fish Fisch
fish (v) fischen
fix (v) reparieren
fizzy sprudelnd
flag Fahne
flashlight Taschenlampe
flavor (n) Geschmack
flea Floh
flight Flug
flower Blume
flu Grippe
fly fliegen
fog Nebel
food Essen
foot Fuß
football Fußball
for für
forbidden verboten
foreign fremd
forget vergessen
fork Gabel
fountain Brunnen
France Frankreich
free (no cost) umsonst

fresh frisch
Friday Freitag
friend Freund
friendship Freundschaft
frisbee Frisbee
from von
fruit Obst
fun Spaß
funeral Beerdigung
funny komisch
furniture Möbel
future Zukunft

G

gallery Galerie
game Spiel
garage Garage
garden Garten
gardening Gärtnern
gas Benzin
gas station Tankstelle
gay schwul
gentleman Herr
genuine echt
Germany Deutschland
gift Geschenk
girl Mädchen
give geben
glass Glas
glasses (eye) Brille
gloves Handschuhe
go gehen
God Gott

gold Gold
golf Golf
good gut
goodbye auf Wiedersehen
good day guten Tag
go through durchgehen
grammar Grammatik
granddaughter Enkelin
grandfather Großvater
grandmother Großmutter
grandson Enkel
gray grau
greasy fettig
great super
Greece Griechenland
green grün
grocery store Lebensmittelgeschäft
guarantee Garantie
guest Gast
guide Führer
guidebook Führer
guitar Gitarre
gum Kaugummi
gun Gewehr

H

hair Haare
hairbrush Haarbürste
haircut Frisur
hand Hand
handicapped behindert
handicrafts Handarbeiten
handiwipes Wischtücher

DICTIONARY

handle (n) Griff
handsome gutaussehend
happy glücklich
harbor Hafen
hard hart
hat Hut
hate (v) hassen
have haben
he er
head Kopf
headache Kopfschmerzen
healthy gesund
hear hören
heart Herz
heat (n) Hitze
heat (v) aufwarmen
heaven Himmel
heavy schwer
hello hallo
helmet Helm
help (n) Hilfe
hemorrhoids Hämorrholden
her ihr
here hier
hi hallo
high hoch
highchair Kinderstuhl
highway Landstraße
hike wandern
hill Hügel
history Geschichte
hitchhike per Anhalter fahren
hobby Hobby
hole Loch

holiday Feiertag
homemade hausgemacht
homesick Heimweh
honest ehrlich
honeymoon Hochzeitsreise
horrible schrecklich
horse Pferd
horse riding reiten
hospital Krankenhaus
hot heiß
hotel Hotel
hour Stunde
house Haus
how many wieviele
how much ($) wieviel kostet
how wie
hungry hungrig
hurry (v) sich beeilen
husband Ehemann
hydrofoil Tragflächenboot

I

I ich
ice Eis
ice cream Eis
ill krank
immediately sofort
important wichtig
imported importiert
impossible unmöglich
in in
included eingeschlossen
incredible unglaublich

independent unabhängig
indigestion Verdauungs-störung
industry Industrie
infection Entzündung
information Information
injured verletzt
innocent unschuldig
insect Insekt
insect repellant Mückenspray
inside innen
instant sofortig
instead anstatt
insurance Versicherung
intelligent klug
interesting interessant
invitation Einladung
iodine Jod
is ist
island Insel
Italy Italien

J

jacket Jacke
jaw Kiefer
jeans Jeans
jewelry Schmuck
job Beruf
jogging Jogging
joke (n) Witz
journey Reise
juice Saft
jump (v) springen

K

keep behalten
kettle Kessel
key Schlüssel
kill töten
kind freundlich
king König
kiss Küß
kitchen Küche
knee Knie
knife Messer
know wissen

L

ladder Leiter
ladies Damen
lake See
lamb Lamm
lamp Lampe
language Sprache
large groß
last letzte
late spät
later später
laugh (v) lachen
laundromat Waschsalon
lawyer Anwalt
lazy faul
leather Leder
leave gehen
left links
leg Bein

lend leihen	**magazine** Zeitschrift
letter Brief	**mail (n)** Post
library Leihbücherei	**main** Haupt
life Leben	**make (v)** machen
light (n) Licht	**male** männlich
light bulb Glühbirne	**man** Mann
lighter (n) Feuerzeug	**manager** Geschäftsführer
like (v) mögen	**many** viele
lip Lippe	**map** Karte
list Liste	**market** Markt
listen zuhören	**married** verheiratet
liter Liter	**matches** Streichhölzer
little (adj) klein	**maximum** Maximum
live leben	**maybe** vielleicht
local örtlich	**meat** Fleisch
lock (n) Schloß	**medicine** Medikamente
lock (v) abschließen	**medium** mittel
lockers Schließfächer	**men** Herren
look gucken	**menu** Speisekarte
lost verloren	**message** Nachricht
loud laut	**metal** Metall
love (v) lieben	**midnight** Mitternacht
lover Liebhaber	**mineral water** Mineralwasser
low niedrig	**minimum** Minimum
lozenges Halsbonbon	**minutes** Minuten
luck Glück	**mirror** Spiegel
luggage Gepäck	**Miss** Fräulein
lukewarm lau	**mistake** Fehler
lungs Lungen	**misunderstanding** Mißverständnis
	mix (n) Mischung
M	**modern** modern
	moment Moment
	Monday Montag
macho macho	**money** Geld
mad wütend	

month Monat
monument Denkmal
moon Mond
more mehr
morning Morgen
mosquito Mücke
mother Mutter
mother-in-law Schwiegermutter
mountain Berg
moustache Schnurrbart
mouth Mund
movie Film
Mr. Herr
Mrs. Frau
much viel
muscle Muskel
museum Museum
music Musik
my mein

N

nail clipper Nagelschere
naked nackt
name Name
napkin Serviette
narrow schmal
nationality Nationalität
natural natürlich
nature Natur
nausea Übelkeit
near nahe
necessary notwendig
necklace Kette

need brauchen
needle Nadel
nephew Neffe
nervous nervös
never nie
new neu
newspaper Zeitung
next nächste
nice nett
nickname Spitzname
niece Nichte
night Nacht
no nein
noisy laut
non-smoking Nichtraucher
noon Mittag
normal normal
north Norden
nose Nase
not nicht
notebook Notizbuch
nothing nichts
no vacancy belegt
now jetzt

O

occupation Beruf
occupied besetzt
ocean Meer
of von
office Büro
O.K. O.K.
old alt

on   auf
once   einmal
one way (street)   einfach
one way (ticket)   Hinfahrkarte
only   nur
open (adj)   offen
open (v)   öffnen
opera   Oper
operator   Vermittlung
optician   Optiker
or   oder
orange (color)   orange
orange (fruit)   Apfelsine
original   Original
other   anderes
outdoors   im Freien
oven   Ofen
over (finished)   beendet
own (v)   besitzen
owner   Besitzer

P

pacifier   Schnuller
package   Paket
page   Seite
pail   Eimer
pain   Schmerz
painting   Gemälde
palace   Schloß
panties   Unterhosen
pants   Hosen
paper   Papier
paper clip   Büroklammer

parents   Eltern
park (v)   parken
park (garden)   Park
party   Party
passenger   Reisende
passport   Paß
pay   bezahlen
peace   Frieden
pedestrian   Fußgänger
pen   Kugelschreiber
pencil   Bleistift
people   Leute
percent   Prozent
perfect   perfekt
perfume   Parfum
period (of time)   Zeitabschnitt
period (woman's)   Periode
person   Person
pet (n)   Haustier
pharmacy   Apotheke
photo   Photo
photocopy   Fotokopie
pick-pocket   Taschendieb
picnic   Picknick
piece   Stück
pig   Schwein
pill   Pille
pillow   Kissen
pin   Nadel
pink   rosa
pity, it's a   wie schade
pizza   Pizza
plane   Flugzeug
plain   einfach

plant Pflanze
plastic Plastik
plastic bag Plastiktüte
plate Teller
platform (train) Bahnsteig
play (v) spielen
play Theater
please bitte
pliers Zange
pocket Tasche
point (v) zeigen
police Polizei
poor arm
pork Schweinefleisch
possible möglich
postcard Postkarte
poster Poster
practical praktisch
pregnant schwanger
prescription Rezept
present (gift) Geschenk
pretty hübsch
price Preis
priest Priester
private privat
problem Problem
profession Beruf
prohibited verboten
pronunciation Aussprache
public öffentlich
pull ziehen
purple violett
purse Handtasche
push drücken

Q

quality Qualität
quarter (¼) Viertel
queen Königin
question (n) Frage
quiet ruhig

R

R.V. Wohnwagen
rabbit Hase
radio Radio
raft Floß
railway Eisenbahn
rain (n) Regen
rainbow Regenbogen
raincoat Regenmantel
rape (n) Vergewaltigung
raw roh
razor Rasierer
ready bereit
receipt Beleg
receive erhalten
receptionist Empfangsperson
recipe Rezept
recommend empfehlen
red rot
refill (v) nachschenken
refund (n) Rückgabe
relax (v) sich erholen
religion Religion
remember sich erinnern
rent (v) mieten

repair (v) reparieren
repeat noch einmal
reservation Reservierung
reserve reservieren
return zurückgeben
rich reich
right rechts
ring (n) Ring
ripe reif
river Fluß
rock (n) Fels
roller skates Rollschuhe
romantic romantisch
roof Dach
room Zimmer
rope Seil
rotten verdorben
roundtrip Rückfahrt
rowboat Ruderboot
rucksack Rucksack
rug Teppich
ruins Ruine
run (v) laufen

S

sad traurig
safe sicher
safety pin Sicherheitsnadel
sailing segeln
sale Ausverkauf
same gleiche
sandals Sandalen
sandwich belegtes Brot

sanitary napkins Damenbinden
Saturday Samstag
scandalous sündig
scarf Schal
school Schule
science Wissenschaft
scientist Wissenschaftler
scissors Schere
scotch tape Tesafilm
screwdriver Schraubenzieher
sculptor Bildhauer
sculpture Skulptur
sea Meer
seafood Meeresfrüchte
seat Platz
second zweite
second class zweiter Klasse
secret Geheimnis
see sehen
self-service Selbstbedienung
sell verkaufen
send senden
separate (adj) getrennt
serious ernsthaft
service Bedienung
sex Sex
sexy sexy
shampoo Shampoo
shaving cream Rasiercreme
she sie
sheet Laken
shell Schale
ship (n) Schiff
ship (v) schicken

shirt   Hemd
shoes   Schuhe
shopping   einkaufen
short   kurz
shorts   shorts
shoulder   Schulter
show (n)   Vorführung
show (v)   zeigen
shower   Dusche
shy   ängstlich
sick   krank
sign   Schild
signature   Unterschrift
silence   Ruhe
silk   Seide
silver   Silber
similar   ähnlich
simple   einfach
sing   singen
singer   Sänger
single   ledig
sink   Waschbecken
sir   mein Herr
sister   Schwester
size   Größe
skating (ice)   Eislaufen
ski (v)   skilaufen
skin   Haut
skinny   dünn
skirt   Rock
sky   Himmel
sleep (v)   schlafen
sleepy   schläfrig
slice   Scheibe

slide (photo)   Dia
slippery   glatt
slow   langsam
small   klein
smell (n)   Geruch
smile (n)   Lächeln
smoking   Rauchen
snack   Imbiß
sneeze (n)   Niesen
snore   schnarchen
snow   Schnee
soap   Seife
soccer   Fußball
socks   Socken
something   etwas
son   Sohn
song   Lied
soon   bald
sorry   Entschuldigung
sour   sauer
south   Süden
speak   sprechen
specialty   Spezialität
speed   Geschwindigkeit
spend   ausgeben
spider   Spinne
spoon   Löffel
sport   Sport
spring   Frühling
square (town)   Platz
stairs   Treppe
stamp   Briefmarke
stapler   Klammeraffe
star (in sky)   Stern

state   Staat
station   Station
stomach   Magen
stop (n)   Halt
stop (v)   halten
storm   Sturm
story (floor)   Stock
straight   geradeaus
strange   merkwürdig
stream (n)   Fluß
street   Straße
strike (no work)   Streik
string   Leine
strong   stark
stuck   festsitzen
student   Student
stupid   dumm
sturdy   haltbar
style   Stil
suddenly   plötzlich
suitcase   Koffer
summer   Sommer
sun   Sonne
sunbathe   sich sonnen
sunburn   Sonnenbrand
Sunday   Sonntag
sunglasses   Sonnenbrille
sunny   sonnig
sunset   Sonnenuntergang
sunscreen   Sonnencreme
sunshine   Sonnenschein
sunstroke   Sonnenstich
suntan (n)   Sonnenbräune
suntan lotion   Sonnenöl

supermarket   Supermarkt
supplement   Zuschlag
surprise (n)   Überraschung
swallow (v)   schlucken
sweat (v)   schwitzen
sweater   Pullover
sweet   süß
swim   schwimmen
swimming pool   Schwimmbad
swim suit   Badeanzug
swim trunks   Badehose
Switzerland   Schweiz
synthetic   synthetisch

T

table   Tisch
tail   Schwanz
take out (food)   mitnehmen
take   nehmen
talcum powder   Babypuder
talk   reden
tall   hoch
tampons   Tampons
tape (cassette)   Kassette
taste (n)   Gaschmack
taste (v)   probieren
tax   Steuer
teacher   Lehrer
team   Team
teenager   Jugendlicher
telephone   Telefon
television   Fernsehen
temperature   Temperatur

tender zart
tennis Tennis
tennis shoes Turnschuhe
tent Zelt
tent pegs Zelthäringe
terrible schrecklich
thanks danke
theater Theater
thermometer Thermometer
they sie
thick dick
thief Dieb
thigh Schenkel
thin dünn
thing Ding
think denken
thirsty durstig
thongs Badelatschen
thread Faden
throat Hals
through durch
throw werfen
Thursday Donnerstag
ticket Eintrittskarte
tight eng
timetable Fahrplan
tired müde
tissues Taschentuch
to nach
today heute
toe Zeh
together zusammen
toilet Toilette
toilet paper Klopapier

tomorrow morgen
tonight heute abend
too zu
tooth Zahn
toothbrush Zahnbürste
toothpaste Zahnpasta
toothpick Zahnstocher
total Völlig
tour Tour
tourist Tourist
towel Handtuch
tower Turm
town Stadt
toy Spielzeug
track (train) Gleis
traditional traditionell
traffic Verkehr
train Zug
translate übersetzen
travel reisen
travel agency Reisebüro
traveler's check Reisescheck
tree Baum
trip Fahrt
trouble Schwierigkeiten
T-shirt T-Shirt
Tuesday Dienstag
tunnel Tunnel
tweezers Pinzette
twins Zwillinge

U

ugly häßlich
umbrella Regenschirm
uncle Onkel
under unter
underpants Unterhose
understand verstehen
underwear Unterwäsche
unemployed arbeitslos
unfortunately unglücklicher-weise
United States Vereinigte Staaten
university Universität
up hoch
upstairs oben
urgent dringend
us uns
use nutzen

V

vacancy (sign) Zimmer frei
vacant frei
valley Tal
vegetarian (n) Vegetarier
very sehr
vest Jacke
video Video
video camera Videokamera
video recorder Videogerät
view Blick
village Dorf
vineyard Weinberg
virus Virus

visit (n) Besuch
visit (v) besuchen
vitamins Vitamine
voice Stimme
vomit (v) sich übergeben

W

waist Taille
wait warten
waiter Kellner
waitress Kellnerin
wake up aufwachen
walk (v) gehen
wallet Brieftasche
want möchte
warm (adj) warm
wash waschen
watch (n) Uhr
watch (v) beobachten
water Wasser
water, tap Leitungswasser
waterfall Wasserfall
we wir
weather Wetter
weather forecast Wettervorhersage
wedding Hochzeit
Wednesday Mittwoch
week Woche
weight Gewicht
welcome willkommen
west Westen
wet naß

what was
wheel Rad
when wann
where wo
whipped cream Schlagsahne
white weiß
white-out Tipp-Ex
who wer
why warum
widow Witwe
widower Witwer
wife Ehefrau
wild wild
wind Wind
window Fenster
wine Wein
wing Flügel
winter Winter
wish (v) wünschen
with mit
without ohne
women Damen
wood Holz
wool Wolle
word Wort

work (n) Arbeit
work (v) arbeiten
world Welt
worse schlechter
worst schlechteste
wrap umwickeln
write schreiben

Y

year Jahr
yellow gelb
yes ja
yesterday gestern
you (formal) Sie
you (informal) du
young jung
youth hostel Jugendherberge

Z

zero null
zip-lock bag Gefrierbeutel
zipper Reißverschluß
zoo Zoo

DICTIONARY

Hurdling the Language Barrier

Don't be afraid to communicate

Even the best phrase book won't satisfy your needs in every situation. To really hurdle the language barrier, you need to leap beyond the printed page, and dive into contact with the locals. Never, never, never allow your lack of foreign language skills to isolate you from the people and cultures you traveled halfway around the world to experience. Remember that in every country you visit, you're surrounded by expert, native-speaking tutors. Spend bus and train rides letting them teach you.

Start conversations by asking politely in the local language, "Do you speak English?" When you speak English with someone from another country, talk slowly, clearly, and with carefully chosen words. Use what the Voice of America calls "simple English." You're talking to people who are wishing it was written down, hoping to see each letter as it tumbles out of your mouth. Pronounce each letter, avoiding all contractions and slang. For bad examples, listen to other tourists.

Keep things caveman-simple. Make single nouns work as entire sentences ("Photo?"). Use internationally-understood words ("Self-service" works in Bavaria). Butcher the language if you must. The important thing is to make the effort. To get air mail stamps, you can flap your wings and say "tweet, tweet." If you want milk, moo and pull two imaginary udders. Risk looking like a fool.

If you're short on words, make your picnic a potluck.

Pull out a map and point out your journey. Draw what you mean. Bring photos from home and introduce your family. Play cards or toss a Frisbee. Fold an origami bird for kids or dazzle 'em with sleight-of-hand magic.

Go ahead and make educated guesses. Many situations are easy-to-fake multiple choice questions. Practice. Read timetables, concert posters and newspaper headlines. Listen to each language on a multilingual tour. Be melodramatic. Exaggerate the local accent. Self-consciousness is the deadliest communication-killer.

Choose multilingual people to communicate with, like students, business people, urbanites, young well-dressed people, or anyone in the tourist trade. Use a small note pad to keep track of handy phrases you pick up—and to help you communicate more clearly with the locals by scribbling down numbers, maps, and so on. Some travelers carry important messages written on a small card (vegetarian, boiled water, your finest ice cream).

Easy cultural bugaboos to avoid:
■ When writing numbers, give your sevens a cross (7) and your ones an upswing (1). European dates are different: Christmas is 25-12-96, not 12-25-96.
■ Commas are decimal points and decimals are commas. A dollar and a half is 1,50 and 5.280 feet are in a mile.
■ The European "first floor" isn't the ground floor, but the first floor up.
■ When counting with your fingers, start with your thumb. If you hold up only your first finger, you'll probably get two of something.

APPENDIX

International words

As our world shrinks, more and more words hop across their linguistic boundaries and become international. Savvy travelers develop a knack for choosing words most likely to be universally understood ("auto" instead of "car," "kaput" rather than "broken," "photo," not "picture"). Internationalize your pronunciation. "University," if you play around with its sound (oo-nee-vehr-see-tay), will be understood anywhere. Practice speaking English with a heavy German accent. Wave your arms a lot. Be creative.

Here are a few internationally understood words. Remember, cut out the Yankee accent and give each word a pan-European sound.

Stop	Kaput	Vino	Restaurant
Ciao	Bank	Hotel	Bye-bye
Rock 'n roll	Post	Camping	OK
Auto	Picnic	Amigo	Autobus (boos)
Nuclear	Macho	Tourist	English
Yankee	Americano	Mama mia	Michelangelo
Beer	Oo la la	Coffee	Casanova (romantic)
Chocolate	Moment	Sexy	Disneyland
Tea	Coca-Cola	No problem	Mañana
Telephone	Photo	Photocopy	Passport
Europa	Self-service	Toilet	Police
Super	Taxi	Central	Information
Pardon	University	Fascist	Rambo
American profanity			

German tongue twisters:

Tongue twisters are a great way to practice a language and break the ice with the locals. Here are a few *Zungenbrecher* that are sure to challenge you, and amuse your hosts:

Zehn zahme Ziegen zogen Zucker zum Zoo.	Ten domesticated goats pulled sugar to the zoo.
Blaukraut bleibt Blaukraut und Brautkleid bleibt Brautkleid.	Bluegrass remains bluegrass and a wedding dress remains a wedding dress.
Fischer's Fritze fischt frische Fische, frische Fische fischt Fischer's Fritze.	Fritz Fischer catches fresh fish, fresh fish Fritz Fisher catches.
Die Katze trapst die Treppe rauf.	The cat is walking up the stairs.
Ich komme über Oberammergau, oder komme ich über Unterammergau?	I am coming via Oberammergau, or am I coming via Unterammergau?

APPENDIX

English tongue twisters:

After your German friends have laughed at you, let them try these tongue twisters in English:

If neither he sells seashells, nor she sells seashells, who shall sell seashells? Shall seashells be sold?	Wenn er keine Muscheln verkauft, und sie verkauft keine Muscheln, wer verkauft dann Muscheln, Werden Muscheln verkauft?
Peter Piper picked a peck of pickled peppers.	Peter Pfeiffer erntete einen Korb voll eingemachter Pfefferschoten.
Rugged rubber baby buggy bumpers.	Starke Gummistoßdämpfer am Kinderwagen.
The sixth sick sheik's sixth sheep's sick.	Das sechste Schaf vom sechsten Scheich ist krank.
Red bug's blood and black bug's blood.	Blut vom roten Käfer und Blut vom schwarzen Käfer.
Soldiers' shoulders.	Soldatenschultern.
Thieves seize skis.	Diebe klauen Schi.
I'm a pleasant mother pheasant plucker. I pluck mother pheasants. I'm the most pleasant mother pheasant plucker that ever plucked a mother pheasant.	Ich bin eine freundliche Federrupferin von Fasanenhennen. Ich rupfe Federn von Fasanenhennen. Ich bin die freundlichste Federrupferin von Fasanenhennen, die je die Federn einer Fasanenhenne gerupft hat.

Let's Talk Telephones

Using die Telefonen

Smart travelers use the telephone every day. It's a snap to make a hotel reservation by phone the morning of the day you plan to arrive. If there's a language problem, ask someone at your hotel to talk to your next hotel for you.

The card-operated public phones are easier to use than coin-operated phones. Buy a *Telefonkarte* (telephone card) at any post office on your first day in a country to force yourself to find smart reasons to use the local phones. Your *Telefonkarte* will work for local, long distance, and international calls made from card-operated public phones throughout that country.

To make calls to other European countries, dial the international access code (00 in Germany, Austria, and Switzerland), followed by the country code (of the country you're calling), followed by the area code without its zero, and finally the local number. When dialing long distance within a country, start with the area code (including its zero), then dial the local number. Post offices have fair, metered long distance phone booths. Public and private phones charge for local calls in eight minute units. If you're calling from a coin-operated phone, don't be surprised if you get cut off without warning.

Calling the USA from any kind of phone is easy if you have an ATT, MCI or SPRINT calling card. Or you can call home using coins (costs $1 for 20 seconds), and ask the other person to call you back at your hotel at a specified

APPENDIX

time. To call Germany from the States, they would dial 011-49-your German area code without the zero-and the local number. Germany-to-USA calls are twice as expensive as direct calls from the States. Midnight in California is breakfast in Berlin.

If you plan to call home often, get an ATT, MCI or SPRINT card. Each card company has a toll-free number in each European country which puts you in touch with an American operator who takes your card number and the number you want to call, puts you through and bills your home phone number for the call (at the cheaper USA rate of about a dollar a minute plus a $2.50 service charge). If you talk for at least 3 minutes, you'll save enough to make up for the service charge.

Hotel room phones are reasonable for local calls, but a terrible rip-off for long-distance calls. Never call home from your hotel room, unless you are using a USA Direct service such as ATT, MCI, or SPRINT. Note that some of the greedier hotels charge even for these "toll-free" calls or have programmed their phones not to accept them. You can avoid this hassle by making your calls from a public phone or the post office.

USA calling card numbers:

Country	ATT	MCI	SPRINT
Germany	0130-0010	0130-0012	0130-0013
Austria	022-903-011	022-903-012	022-903-014
Switzerland	155-00-11	155-02-22	155-97-77

International access codes:
These are the numbers you dial first when calling out of a country.

Germany:	00
Austria:	00
Switzerland:	00
U.S.A.:	011

Country codes:
After you've dialed the international access code, then dial the code of the country you're calling.

Austria:	43	Germany:	49	Portugal:	351
Belgium:	32	Greece:	30	Spain:	34
Britain:	44	Hungary:	36	Sweden:	46
Czech Rep.:	42	Italy:	39	Switzerland:	41
Denmark:	45	Netherlands:	31	Turkey:	90
France:	33	Norway:	47	USA/Canada:	1

APPENDIX

Weather

First line is average daily low (°F.); second line average daily high (°F.); third line, days of no rain.

	J	F	M	A	M	J	J	A	S	O	N	D
GERMANY	29	31	35	41	48	53	56	55	51	43	36	31
Frankfurt	37	42	49	58	67	72	75	74	67	56	45	39
	22	19	22	21	22	21	21	21	21	22	21	20
AUSTRIA	26	28	34	41	50	56	59	58	52	44	36	30
Vienna	34	38	47	57	66	71	75	73	66	55	44	37
	23	21	24	21	22	21	22	21	23	23	22	22
SWITZ.	29	30	35	41	48	55	58	57	52	44	37	31
Geneva	39	43	51	58	66	73	77	76	69	58	47	40
	20	19	21	19	19	19	22	21	20	20	19	21

Metric conversions (approximate)

1 inch = 25 millimeters   1 foot = .3 meter
1 yard = .9 meter   1 mile = 1.6 kilometers
1 sq. yard = .8 sq. meter   1 acre = 0.4 hectare
1 quart = .95 liter   1 ounce = 28 grams
1 pound = .45 kilo   1 kilo = 2.2 pounds
1 centimeter = 0.4 inch   1 meter = 39.4 inches
1 kilometer = .62 mile
Miles = kilometers divided by 2 plus 10%
(120 km ÷ 2 = 60, 60 +12 = 72 miles)
Fahrenheit degrees = double Celsius + 30
32° F = 0° C, 82° F = about 28° C

Your tear-out cheat sheet

Good day.	**Guten Tag.**	**goo**-ten tahg
Do you speak English?	**Sprechen Sie Englisch?**	**shprekh**-en zee **eng**-lish
Yes. / No.	**Ja. / Nein.**	yah / nīn
I don't speak German.	**Ich spreche kein Deutsch.**	ikh **shprekh**-eh kīn doych
I'm sorry.	**Entschuldigung.**	ent-**shool**-dee-goong
Please. / Thank you.	**Bitte. / Danke.**	**bit**-teh / **dahng**-keh
No problem.	**Kein Problem.**	kīn proh-**blaym**
Very good.	**Sehr gut.**	zehr goot
You are very kind.	**Sie sind sehr freundlich.**	zee zint zehr **froynd**-likh
Goodbye.	**Auf Wiedersehen.**	owf **vee**-der-zayn
Where is...?	**Wo ist...?**	voh ist
...a hotel	**...ein Hotel**	īn hoh-**tel**
...a youth hostel	**...eine Jugend- herberge**	ī-neh **yoo**-gend- hehr-behr-geh
...a restaurant	**...ein Restaurant**	īn res-tow-**rahnt**
...a supermarket	**...ein Supermarkt**	īn **zoo**-per-markt
...a pharmacy	**...eine Apotheke**	ī-neh ah-poh-**tay**-keh
...a bank	**...eine Bank**	ī-neh bahnk
...the train station	**...der Bahnhof**	dehr **bahn**-hohf
...the tourist information office	**...das Touristen- informationsbüro**	dahs **too**-ris-ten-in-for- maht-see-**ohns**-bew-roh
...the toilet	**...die Toilette**	dee toh-**leh**-teh

men / women	**Herren / Damen**	**hehr**-ren / **dah**-men
How much is it?	**Wieviel kostet das?**	vee-**feel kos**-tet dahs
Write it?	**Schreiben?**	**shrī**-ben
Cheap / Cheaper /	**Billig / Billiger /**	**bil**-lig / **bil**-lig-er /
Cheapest.	**Am Billigsten.**	ahm **bil**-lig-sten
Is it free?	**Ist es umsonst?**	ist es oom-**zohnst**
Included?	**Eingeschlossen?**	**īn**-geh-shlos-sen
Do you have...?	**Haben Sie...?**	**hah**-ben zee
I would like...	**Ich hätte gern...**	ikh **het**-teh gehrn
We would like...	**Wir hätten gern...**	veer **het**-ten gehrn
...this.	**...dies.**	deez
...just a little.	**...nur ein bißchen.**	noor īn **bis**-yen
...more.	**...mehr.**	mehr
...a ticket.	**...ein Karte.**	īn **kar**-teh
...a room.	**...ein Zimmer.**	īn **tsim**-mer
...the bill.	**...die Rechnung.**	dee **rekh**-noong
one	**eins**	īns
two	**zwei**	tsvī
three	**drei**	drī
four	**vier**	feer
five	**fünf**	fewnf
six	**sechs**	zex
seven	**sieben**	**zee**-ben
eight	**acht**	ahkht
nine	**neun**	noyn
ten	**zehn**	tsayn
At what time?	**Um wieviel Uhr?**	oom vee-**feel** oor
Just a moment.	**Moment.**	moh-**ment**
now / soon / later	**jetzt / bald / später**	yetzt / bahld / **shpay**-ter
today / tomorrow	**heute / morgen**	**hoy**-teh / **mor**-gen

Faxing your hotel reservation

Most hotel managers know basic "hotel English." Use this handy form for your fax.

. . . .

One page fax   My fax #:_____
To: Today's date: ____ / ____ / ____
From: day   month   year
Dear Hotel _____,
   Please make this reservation for me:

Name: _____
Total # of people: ____   # of rooms: ____   # of nights: ____

Arriving: ____ / ____ / ____   Time of arrival (24-hour clock): _____
      day   month   year   (I will telephone if later)
Departing: ____ / ____ / ____
      day   month   year

Room(s): Single   Double   Twin   Triple   Quad   Quint
With: Toilet   Shower   Bath   Sink only
Special needs: View   Quiet   Cheapest room   Ground floor
Credit card: Visa   Mastercard   American Express

Card #: _____   Exp. date: _____
Name on card: _____

If a deposit is necessary, you may charge me for the first night. Please fax or mail me confirmation of my reservation, the type of room reserved, the price, and if the price includes breakfast. Thank you.

Signed: _____   Phone: _____
Address: _____

Rick Steves' Europe Through the Back Door Catalog

All of these items have been specially designed for independent budget travelers. They have been thoroughly field tested by Rick Steves and his globe-trotting ETBD staff, and are completely guaranteed. Prices include shipping, tax, and a free subscription to Rick's quarterly newsletter/catalog.

Back Door Bag convertible suitcase/backpack $75

At 9"x21"x13" this specially-designed, sturdy, functional bag is maximum carry-on-the-plane size (fits under the seat), and your key to foot-loose and fancy-free travel. Made in the USA from rugged, water-resistant 1000 denier Cordura nylon, it converts from a smart-looking suitcase to a handy backpack. It has hide-away padded shoulder straps, top and side handles, and a detachable shoulder strap (for toting as a suitcase). Beefy, lockable perimeter zippers allow easy access to the roomy (2500 cubic inches) main compartment. Two large outside pockets are perfect for frequently used items. A nylon stuff bag is also included. Over 50,000 Back Door travelers have used these bags around the world. Rick Steves helped design this bag, and lives out of it for 3 months at a time. Comparable bags cost much more. Available in black, grey, navy blue and très chic teal green.

European railpasses

...cost the same everywhere, but only ETBD gives you a free hour-long "How to get the most out of your railpass" video, free advice on your itinerary, and your choice of one of Rick Steves' regional "Best of..." guidebooks. For starters, call 206/771-8303, and we'll send you a free copy of Rick Steves' Annual Guide to European Railpasses.

Moneybelt $8

Absolutely required no matter where you're traveling! An ultra-light, sturdy, under-the-pants, one-size-fits-all nylon pouch, our svelte moneybelt is just the right size to carry your passport, airline tickets and traveler's checks comfortably. Made to ETBD's exacting specifications, this moneybelt is your best defense against theft—when you wear it, feeling a street urchin's hand in your pocket becomes just another interesting cultural experience.

Prices include shipping within the USA/Canada, and are good through 1995—maybe longer. Orders will be processed within 2 weeks. For rush orders (which we process within 48 hours), please add $10. Washington residents please add 8.2% sales tax. Send your check to:

Rick Steves' Europe Through the Back Door
120 Fourth Ave. N, PO Box 2009
Edmonds, WA 98020

More books by Rick Steves...

Now more than ever, travelers are determined to get the most out of every mile, minute and dollar. That's what Rick's books are all about. He'll help you have a better trip because you're on a budget, not in spite of it. Each of these books is published by John Muir Publications, and is available through your local bookstore, or through Rick's free Europe Through the Back Door newsletter/catalog.

Rick Steves' Europe Through The Back Door

Updated every year, *ETBD* has given thousands of people the skills and confidence they needed to travel through the less-touristed "back doors" of Europe. You'll find chapters on packing, itinerary-planning, transportation, finding rooms, travel photography, keeping safe and healthy, plus chapters on Rick's favorite back door discoveries.

Mona Winks: Self-Guided Tours of Europe's Top Museums

Let's face it, museums can ruin a good vacation. But *Mona* takes you by the hand, giving you fun and easy-to-follow self-guided tours through Europe's 20 most frightening and exhausting museums and cultural obligations. Packed with more than 200 maps and illustrations.

Europe 101: History and Art for the Traveler

A lively, entertaining crash course in European history and art, *101* is the perfect way to prepare yourself for the rich cultural smorgasbord that awaits you.

Rick Steves' Best of Germany, Austria & Switzerland
Rick Steves' Best of Europe
Rick Steves' Best of Great Britain
Rick Steves' Best of France, Belgium & the Netherlands
Rick Steves' Best of Italy
Rick Steves' Best of Scandinavia
Rick Steves' Best of Spain & Portugal
Rick Steves' Best of the Baltics & Russia

For a successful trip, raw information isn't enough. In his *Best of...* guides, Rick Steves weeds through each region's endless possibilities to give you candid, straightforward advice on what to see, where to sleep, how to manage your time, and how to get the most out of every dollar. Rick personally updates these guides every year.

Rick Steves' European Phrase Books: French, Italian, German, Spanish/Portuguese, and French/Italian/German

Finally, a series of phrase books written especially for the budget traveler! Each book gives you the words and phrases you need to communicate with the locals about room-finding, transportation, food, health—you'll even learn how to start conversations about politics, philosophy and romance—all spiced with Rick Steves' travel tips, and his unique blend of down-to-earth practicality and humor. All are 1995 editions.

What we do at Europe Through the Back Door

At ETBD we value travel as a powerful way to better understand and contribute to the world in which we live. Our mission at ETBD is to equip travelers with the confidence and skills necessary to travel through Europe independently, economically, and in a way that is culturally broadening. To accomplish this, we:

■ Teach budget European travel skills seminars (often for free);

■ Research and write guidebooks to Europe;

■ Write and host a Public Television series;

■ Sell European railpasses, our favorite guidebooks, maps, travel bags, and travel accessories;

■ Provide European travel consulting services;

■ Organize and lead free-spirited Back Door tours of Europe, France, Italy, Turkey, and beyond;

■ Run a Travel Resource Center in espresso-correct Edmonds, WA;

...and we travel a lot.

Back Door 'Best of Europe' tours

If you like our independent travel philosophy but would like to benefit from the camaraderie and efficiency of group travel, our Back Door tours may be right up your alley. Every year we lead friendly, intimate 'Best of Europe in 22 Days' tours, free-spirited 'Bus, Bed & Breakfast' tours, and special regional tours of Turkey, Britain, France, and other fun places. For details, call 206/771-8303 and ask for our free newsletter/catalog.

Other Books from
John Muir Publications

Travel Books by Rick Steves
**Asia Through the Back Door,
4th ed.,** 400 pp. $16.95
**Europe 101: History, Art, and
Culture for the Traveler,
4th ed.,** 372 pp. $15.95
**Mona Winks: Self-Guided Tours
of Europe's Top Museums,
2nd ed.,** 456 pp. $16.95
**Rick Steves' Best of the Baltics
and Russia, 1995 ed.** 144 pp.
$9.95
**Rick Steves' Best of Europe,
1995 ed.,** 544 pp. $16.95
**Rick Steves' Best of France,
Belgium, and the Netherlands,
1995 ed.,** 240 pp. $12.95
**Rick Steves' Best of Germany,
Austria, and Switzerland, 1995
ed.,** 240 pp. $12.95
**Rick Steves' Best of Great
Britain, 1995 ed.,** 192 pp.
$11.95
**Rick Steves' Best of Italy, 1995
ed.,** 208 pp. $11.95
**Rick Steves' Best of
Scandinavia, 1995 ed.,**
192 pp. $11.95

**Rick Steves' Best of Spain and
Portugal, 1995 ed.,** 192 pp.
$11.95
**Rick Steves' Europe Through
the Back Door, 13th ed.,**
480 pp. $17.95
**Rick Steves' French Phrase
Book, 2nd ed.,** 112 pp. $4.95
**Rick Steves' German Phrase
Book, 2nd ed.,** 112 pp. $4.95
**Rick Steves' Italian Phrase
Book, 2nd ed.,** 112 pp. $4.95
**Rick Steves' Spanish and
Portuguese Phrase Book, 2nd
ed.,** 288 pp. $5.95
**Rick Steves' French/German/
Italian Phrase Book,** 288 pp.
$6.95

*European Travel Titles For
Young Readers
Ages 8 & Up*
**Kidding Around London,
2nd ed.,** 64 pp., $9.95
**Kidding Around Paris,
2nd ed.,** 64 pp., $9.95
Kidding Around Spain,
108 pp. $12.95